I0186717

DECLUTTER YOUR HOME

A STEP-BY-STEP GUIDE TO ORGANIZE EVERY ROOM, MAXIMIZE SPACE, INCREASE PRODUCTIVITY, REDUCE STRESS, AND FALL IN LOVE WITH YOUR HOME AGAIN

WHITNEY WILLARD

© **Copyright 2025 - All rights reserved.**

The content contained within this book may not be reproduced, duplicated or transmitted without direct written permission from the author or the publisher.

Under no circumstances will any blame or legal responsibility be held against the publisher, or author, for any damages, reparation, or monetary loss due to the information contained within this book, either directly or indirectly.

Legal Notice:

This book is copyright protected. It is only for personal use. You cannot amend, distribute, sell, use, quote or paraphrase any part, or the content within this book, without the consent of the author or publisher.

Disclaimer Notice:

Please note the information contained within this document is for educational and entertainment purposes only. All effort has been executed to present accurate, up to date, reliable, complete information. No warranties of any kind are declared or implied. Readers acknowledge that the author is not engaged in the rendering of legal, financial, medical or professional advice. The content within this book has been derived from various sources. Please consult a licensed professional before attempting any techniques outlined in this book.

By reading this document, the reader agrees that under no circumstances is the author responsible for any losses, direct or indirect, that are incurred as a result of the use of the information contained within this document, including, but not limited to, errors, omissions, or inaccuracies.

Meridian Hills Publishing

Hardcover ISBN: 979-8-89754-002-0

Paperback ISBN: 979-8-89754-001-3

E-Book ISBN: 979-8-89754-000-6

CONTENTS

INTRODUCTION

Have you ever found yourself feeling overwhelmed by the sheer amount of stuff in your home? That feeling of chaos and clutter that seep into every corner of your life can be more than just an inconvenience. It can drain your energy, make it difficult to relax, and even impact your mental well-being, productivity, and relationships. The clutter doesn't just create a visual mess; it can act like an invisible weight that affects your mood, focus, and sense of peace. Whether it's the pile of papers on your desk, the ever-growing stack of clothes in your bedroom, or the disorganized kitchen that's hard to cook in, the constant presence of clutter can easily make you feel like you're always playing catch-up. But what if I told you there was a way to break free from this cycle? What if you could create a space that not only supports your daily needs but also uplifts your energy and makes you feel at ease every time you walk through the door?

In *Declutter Your Home*, we're going to look into how clutter impacts not only the physical space you live in but also how it can affect every aspect of your life. By understanding the connections between your physical environment and your mental state, we'll explore how clearing out the clutter can lead to a more organized, balanced, and fulfilling life. Physical clutter often consists of unused items or disorganization. It can also contribute to mental clutter, stress, and distractions. These mental barriers can prevent you from feeling calm and focused, leading to a sense of overwhelm that's hard to shake off. This cycle can lead to frustration, anxiety, and a constant feeling of being "behind" in every aspect of your life. But here's the good news: you don't have to live this way. It's entirely possible to regain control over your space, clear out the clutter, and create an environment that truly nurtures and supports you.

The first step toward this transformation is setting realistic goals. Many people make the mistake of trying to tackle their clutter all at once, often leading to burnout or discouragement. A successful decluttering journey starts with intentionality and manageable steps. Setting achievable goals, prevents overwhelm and keeps you on track. It's important to remember that this process is a marathon, not a sprint. Rather than tackling your entire house in one weekend, focus on one room or area at a time. Each small win builds momentum, making your space work for you rather than against you. The sense of accomplishment and relief that comes with clearing away even a small area of clutter can have a profound impact on your overall mood and motivation.

In this book, we will guide you through every step of the decluttering process, from understanding your clutter to putting practical, actionable solutions into place. You will gain insights into how your physical environment affects your mental state, and we'll explore how you can tackle your clutter in a way that reduces stress and helps you feel more in control of your life. Through each chapter, we'll introduce you to techniques, strategies, and exercises that will make your decluttering journey smoother, more efficient, and more sustainable. Decluttering isn't just a one-time deep clean—it's about lasting changes that maintain organization over time.

We begin by exploring the roots of clutter, examining not just the stuff that piles up but also the emotional and psychological aspects that contribute to it. Often, we hold onto things for sentimental reasons, out of guilt, or because we feel that we might need them "someday." By understanding these emotional attachments, we can make better decisions about what to keep, what to donate, and what to discard. You'll also learn how to assess the current state of your home and prioritize areas based on their use and impact on your daily life. This book will create a personalized plan for tackling clutter, and you'll learn how to break down the overwhelming task into bite-sized, achievable goals.

Each chapter in this book is designed to guide you through specific areas of your home, offering practical tips and exercises for decluttering every room, from the living room to the kitchen, bedroom, bathroom, and office. We'll show you how to maximize your space, boost your productivity, and create a space that encourages relaxation and peace of mind. For example, you'll learn how to organize your kitchen so that meal preparation becomes a breeze, how to create a restful retreat in your bedroom, and how to streamline your home office for maximum efficiency. The goal isn't just to clean up; it's about creating a home that enhances your quality of life and reflects the person you want to be.

Whether you're working from home, caring for a family, or juggling a busy lifestyle, this book is designed to fit into your daily routine. We know that time is precious, and we want to make sure that the decluttering process doesn't add to your stress. By focusing on one step at a time and incorporating small, consistent changes into your routine, you'll see a gradual, sustainable transformation. The exercises and strategies in this book will help you create healthy habits that support ongoing organization so you won't have to worry about your home falling into disarray again.

By the end of this journey, you'll not only have a clutter-free home but also a sense of accomplishment, clarity, and peace. You'll find that decluttering isn't just about cleaning up; it's about creating a space that fosters well-being and makes room for the things that truly matter in your life. You'll be amazed at how much lighter and freer you feel when your environment is organized and supportive of your goals. You'll gain mental clarity, feel more focused, and experience a renewed sense of joy in your space.

So, let's get started on this journey together. With each step, you'll find yourself moving closer to the home of your dreams. It will be a home that not only looks beautiful but also supports your lifestyle, reduces stress, and helps you fall in love with your space again. You've got this!

1

THE MINDSET SHIFT-DECLUTTERING STARTS WITH YOU

W elcome to the first step in transforming your home into a space that feels calm, organized, and truly yours. Before we look into the nuts and bolts of decluttering your home, let's pause and focus on something equally important—your mindset. How you approach decluttering matters just as much as the physical act of organizing. If you're like most people, clutter can feel like a never-ending battle. But I promise you, it's not.

Decluttering isn't just about throwing things away; it's about embracing simplicity, intentionality, and peace. Imagine walking into a room where everything has its place—no more shifting clutter to find what you need. How would that make you feel? Calm? Focused? Empowered?

That's the magic of decluttering, but it starts with shifting the way you think about your space and your belongings.

Looking at a cluttered home can feel overwhelming. If you're a busy professional, a parent, an entrepreneur, or someone working from home, time is precious. That's why decluttering can seem like a luxury you don't have. Here's the truth: decluttering isn't about spending hours or creating a Pinterest-perfect home. Instead, it's about making small but impactful changes that make a big difference in how you feel.

The key is to start small, stay consistent, and embrace the process. A clean, organized home doesn't happen overnight, but with the right mindset, it's completely achievable—without the stress. So, are you ready?

Let's start by exploring the first step: Identifying emotional attachments to possessions.

IDENTIFYING EMOTIONAL ATTACHMENTS TO POSSESSIONS

One of the biggest obstacles when it comes to decluttering is our emotional attachment to belongings. You may hold onto items that no longer serve you simply because of the memories or feelings they evoke. That's okay. It's completely natural. Here's the thing: Emotions can often cloud your judgment, making it harder to let go of things that no longer add value to your life.

Take a moment and think about your closet or that overflowing drawer in your kitchen. How many items do you hold onto because they remind you of a special moment, person, or time in your life?

Maybe it's the sweater from a vacation, the book you were gifted by a dear friend, or the trinket from a past relationship. While these items once held meaning, over time, they can become emotional baggage, weighing you down both physically and mentally.

Consider this scenario: Imagine you have a box of old clothes that you haven't worn in years, filled with items from different chapters of your life, some you don't even remember buying. Each piece tells a story, but that doesn't mean you have to keep it. Often, we hang onto things because we're afraid of losing the memories attached to them. But the reality is that the memory is in your mind, not in the object.

A friend of mine, Nina, had a closet full of clothes she hadn't worn in years. She kept them because each item reminded her of a special moment in her past: her wedding day, her college graduation, or her first big job interview. But as she started her decluttering journey, she realized that holding on to these clothes didn't keep those memories alive. The memories were hers to cherish; the clutter only weighed her down. Once she let go of the clothes, she felt lighter and more connected to the present rather than stuck in the past.

Consider the digital clutter as well—old emails, photos, or files you've saved "just in case." Every time you open your inbox or scroll through your phone, you're reminded of those attachments, be it the emails from your old job or the 300 photos you've never bothered to organize. They take up valuable mental space and energy, preventing you from truly focusing on the present.

Asking yourself the right questions can help. Try these:

- Do I really need this to feel good about myself?
- Will letting go of this object free up my space and mental energy?

Once you accept that memories aren't tied to objects, decluttering becomes easier.

It's essential to approach the process of decluttering with compassion for yourself. The emotional attachment to possessions isn't something that will disappear overnight. It's a gradual process that requires reflection, mindfulness, and patience.

As you go through this journey, remind yourself that each item you part with is an opportunity to create room for things that truly matter. By understanding your emotional attachments, you can let go, make space for new experiences, and ultimately create a home that works for you—not the other way around.

OVERCOMING COMMON MENTAL BLOCKS IN DECLUTTERING

Now that you've identified your emotional attachments to possessions, let's focus on the mental blocks that often hold us back from decluttering. Although letting go of sentimental items is tough, there are other common psychological hurdles you'll face along the way. These mental blocks can make decluttering feel overwhelming, but recognizing them is the first step toward overcoming them.

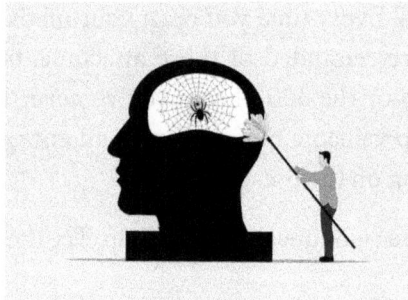

The Fear of Future Regret: Holding Onto "What-ifs"

One of the most significant mental blocks you'll encounter when decluttering is the belief that you *need* to keep everything. You've probably thought, "What if I need this later?" or "I will regret getting rid of this." It's a fear-based mindset, and very natural to feel it when you've been surrounded by things for a long time (Burkeman, 2017).

This fear of regret is real, especially for things you rarely use but still feel you might "need" someday.

Take, for example, that pile of old electronics. Cables, chargers, and outdated gadgets pile up because you haven't been able to toss them out. Why? Maybe you're holding onto the hope that one day you'll find a use for them, or you're worried about the environmental impact of throwing them away. Holding onto "what-ifs" clutters your space and bogs down your mind with unnecessary worry.

The Guilt Factor: Letting Go of Sentimental Items

Another common mental block is *guilt.* Many of us feel guilty about parting with items that were gifts, inherited, or purchased with hard-earned money. The guilt often stems from a sense of obligation to keep something because someone else gave it to you or because it cost a significant amount. Here's the truth: You don't have to hold onto things out of guilt. Gifts and purchases are expressions of love or choices from a different time in your life, and if they no longer serve you, they can be released with gratitude.

For instance, think about a beautiful vase your aunt gave you. You've moved houses several times, and it's been collecting dust in the back of a cupboard. Every time you come across it, you feel a pang of guilt because she gave it to you with such care. Ask yourself: Does it fit your home and bring you joy? If the answer is no, it might be time to let go of the guilt and pass it along to someone who might appreciate it more.

The Perfectionism Trap: Getting Stuck in the Process

Then there's the *perfectionism* trap. You can find yourself stuck in the process because you think every item has to be perfectly categorized or neatly organized before you can move on. This perfectionist mindset can leave you feeling paralyzed, thinking that if it's not done right, it's not worth doing at all. The truth is, there is no "perfect" way to declutter; what matters is starting and making progress, no matter how small.

Perfectionism often pops up when you're trying to organize an area that's been neglected for a while. Maybe it's an overstuffed closet or a spare room that's become a storage dumping ground. You can feel overwhelmed by the thought of it all, thinking it has to be perfectly done in one go. But remember, decluttering is a journey, not a sprint. You can always revisit areas later as your needs and your space evolve.

Attachment to the Past: Letting Go of Physical Memories

One of the trickier mental blocks is the feeling of *attachment to the past*. We often hold onto things because they remind us of a different time in our lives. These items can be childhood toys, a letter from an old friend, or clothes we wore during a special event. They represent memories, milestones, or relationships that may not be in our lives anymore. But the more we hold on to physical representations of the past, the harder it becomes to move forward.

For example, you may have a box of old journals or diaries from your teenage years. As you flip through the pages, you're flooded with memories of high school, friendships, and dreams you had back then. But those journals don't need to take up valuable space in your home to keep those memories alive. Instead, find ways to store the memories in your heart and mind, letting go of the physical items that no longer serve you.

Overwhelm: Breaking the Task into Manageable Chunks

Finally, being overwhelmed is a huge mental block that can leave you feeling stuck before you even begin. The sheer thought of decluttering can seem like an insurmountable task, especially when it involves multiple rooms or areas in your home. You might think, "Where do I even start?" or "This will take forever." But the truth is, decluttering doesn't have to be an all-or-nothing endeavor. Start small, break it into manageable chunks, and focus on one area at a time.

Perhaps it's just tackling the junk drawer in your kitchen or clearing the clutter from the dining table. Once you finish, you'll feel a sense of accomplishment, and the next area will seem less overwhelming. You don't need to declutter your entire home in one weekend. Taking things step by step will help you gain momentum without feeling crushed by the weight of it all.

With these mental blocks behind you, it's time to take action. Start by decluttering and organizing your home by first visualizing your ideal living space. When you can clearly picture how you want your home to feel, it becomes easier to make decisions about what stays and what goes.

Let's learn three practical exercises that will help you envision and create that space.

Exercise 1: The "Room by Room" Visioning Exercise

Focus on one room at a time. Tackling your entire home all at once can feel overwhelming, but breaking it down into smaller chunks makes the process much more manageable. Here's how you can do it:

1. **Pick a room:** Pick a room where you spend the most time or one that you feel would have the biggest positive impact once organized. Maybe it's your living room, home office, or bedroom.
2. **Close your eyes:** Take a deep breath, then close your eyes and picture that room in its most ideal state.
   a. What does it look like?
   b. Is it clutter-free, with the essentials neatly arranged?
   c. Does it have a cozy feeling, with your favorite items perfectly placed?
3. **Imagine the details:** Go deeper into the visualization.
   a. How does the room feel when you walk in?
   b. What colors do you see? What is it lit?
   c. Is there a place for everything? Make your vision as specific as possible. If you can picture it clearly, it will be easier to bring it to life.
4. **Write it down:** Open your eyes and jot down a description of the room.
   a. What's working in your vision, and what's not? Write

down any areas that need attention or things that you'd like to change. This step will serve as your guiding map.

Exercise 2: The "Lifestyle Fit" Visualization

Now that you've envisioned a specific room, consider how it fits your lifestyle. Decluttering isn't just about tidying up—it's about shaping your home to fit your life. This exercise will help you ensure your space is both functional and supportive of your needs.

1. **Consider your daily routine:** How do you use the space? For example, in your home office, is your desk piled with papers, or do you prefer a clean, organized space? Is your bedroom a restful retreat, or does clutter add to your stress?
2. **Visualize how it supports your life:** how this space could better support your life once organized. Picture yourself in the room, completing tasks with ease, feeling calm and productive. Would a more streamlined layout help you get more work done or make it easier to unwind?
3. **Identify what needs to go:** What items don't support the feel or function you want?" These are the things you can let go of.

Exercise 3: The "Emotional Connection" Visualization

Finally, focus on how you *want* your home to make you feel. Successful decluttering relies heavily on your emotions. Surrounding yourself with uplifting items helps you feel more inspired and energized in your space.

1. **Consider your ideal emotional state:** How do you want to feel when you step into a room? Calm, energized, inspired, or organized? This emotional connection will guide you in deciding what stays.
2. **Visualize your emotional response:** Picture yourself in the room—how does it make you feel? Do you feel motivated and happy in that space? If not, what's causing that emotional

disconnect? It could be too much stuff, cluttered surfaces, or items that no longer serve a purpose.

3. **Align your belongings with your feelings:** Mentally scan the room and assess the emotional connection you have with each item.

   a. Does that old stack of papers spark joy or create stress?

   b. Does that unused piece of exercise equipment motivate you or just take up space? It's all about aligning your possessions with the feelings you want to nurture in your home.

Now that you understand your emotional connections to your possessions, it's time to assess your home and create a customized plan that works for you. The next chapter will walk you through how to prioritize areas of your home that need attention based on both their function and the impact they have on your daily life. This process is all about turning your goals into a tangible, manageable action plan.

2

CREATING A PERSONALIZED DECLUTTERING PLAN

I t's the weekend, and today's the day. You've decided you are going to tackle the clutter in your home that's been nagging at you for months, maybe even longer. You wake up feeling motivated, grab a coffee, and stare at the mess around you. A pile of laundry that's been sitting on the couch for a week. The stacks of papers are scattered across the kitchen counter. The closet that's bursting at the seams with clothes you haven't worn in years. An hour ago you were energized. Now you feel overwhelmed. Where do you even start?

You sit down, take a deep breath, and realize that if you want real progress, you need a plan. Not just any plan—one that's tailored to *your* space, your needs, and your lifestyle. Let's face it, decluttering isn't a one-size-fits-all process. It's not about following some generic checklist you found online; it's about creating a strategy that will work for you in the long-term.

This is where this chapter comes in. It's time to break things down and create a personalized decluttering plan that fits into your busy life. No more jumping in headfirst without a clear goal. No more overwhelm. It's time to take control—one room at a time, in a way that feels sustainable and manageable.

ASSESSING YOUR HOME'S CURRENT STATE

Before decluttering, take stock of where you are right now. This step helps you assess your home's current state and what's working and what's not. With a clear picture of the situation, you can make informed decisions about what to keep, what to toss, and what to donate.

Start With a Walkthrough

Don't rush. Walk through each room with fresh eyes. As you walk through your space, try to see things from a new perspective. Look beyond what's physically there—consider how those items make you feel.

Think about how each room functions for you.

- Does it support your lifestyle?
- Is it just holding on to things that no longer serve you?
- Is your living room a relaxing space, or is it filled with old magazines and cluttered shelves that make you feel stressed?
- If you work from home, is your office truly conducive to productivity?
- Is it filled with stacks of paper and unorganized files?

Consider the Emotional Impact of Clutter

Emotions shape how we relate to our living spaces.

Do some rooms feel welcoming, or do they feel like a constant source of stress?

A cluttered desk drains your productivity, while a disorganized kitchen turns meal prep into a frustrating chore. Even small items—like a pile of unopened mail or an overflowing laundry basket—can contribute to a sense of overwhelm. Taking note of these emotional triggers is critical in understanding what needs to change.

For example, if your bedroom feels chaotic due to the clutter on your nightstand, start. Even small visual clutter can create mental clutter. That's why it's so important to evaluate how your space impacts you on an emotional level.

Check for Hidden Clutter

Often, clutter isn't always visible at first glance. Check hidden spaces —drawers, closets, and under the bed—where items tend to pile up and go unnoticed. A drawer full of old receipts or a closet stuffed with unworn clothes might be easy to ignore, but they're silently adding to your clutter problem.

As you sort through these areas, ask yourself how often do I use them.

1. Are those items adding value to your life?
2. Are they just occupying space because it's easier to leave them there than to sort through them?

A cluttered closet drains more mental energy than you realize because every time you open the door, you're reminded that it's disorganized.

Prioritize the Problem Areas

After your walkthrough, take note of the spaces that are causing you the most stress. Maybe it's your kitchen counter covered in miscellaneous items or your home office turned dumping ground for things you don't know where to put. Tackling these problem areas will make the biggest impact.

Here's a trick: List the most frustrating spaces and rank them in order of urgency. For example:

- **Living room:** Overstuffed couch with laundry, papers scattered on the coffee table.
- **Kitchen:** Countertops cluttered with random kitchen gadgets and junk mail.
- **Bedroom:** Clothes on the floor and items on the nightstand make it feel crowded.

Pinpointing the "worst offender" can help you focus your energy on the areas that will bring the most satisfaction once they're decluttered.

Take a Visual Inventory

To avoid overlooking clutter, take photos of the spaces you want to declutter. Sometimes, seeing the space in pictures often reveals how clutter is taking over. It can also help you visualize the potential for change. Snap pictures of the rooms you're struggling with and revisit them after a few days. You may find that your assessment changes as you start to see the space differently with fresh eyes.

Evaluate Functionality

After assessing the visual state of your home, think about func-tionality.

- Does your space work for you?
- Do you have a space designated for all of your daily activities, or are things scattered around wherever they fit?

Decluttering isn't just about tidiness—it's also about creating a func-tional and stress-free environment.

For example, if your kitchen is cluttered, but it's also where you prepare meals, cleaning the counters will make it more conducive to cooking. A messy closet makes it hard to find your clothes, but an organized one can make your mornings run smoother.

Now that you've assessed your home's current state, you have a clearer understanding of what needs to change. You've identified the most stressful areas and discovered how to make your space work for you. This is the foundation of your personalized decluttering plan. By taking stock of what you have, how it impacts your life, and what's truly necessary, you can begin to craft a plan that will bring real transformation to your home.

PRIORITIZING AREAS BASED ON USE AND IMPACT

Now, it's time to take things a step further by prioritizing the areas that need attention. This step focuses your energy on the spaces that will make the most difference in your daily life. You don't have to tackle everything at once, and that's okay. By strategically selecting the most impactful areas, you'll begin to feel a shift in your home's atmosphere more quickly.

Prioritizing Areas Based on Use and Impact

Decluttering can feel overwhelming, especially when you're juggling multiple responsibilities. But here's the good news: You don't need to do everything at once. Consider how often you use each room and how much impact the clutter in those spaces has on your daily life. Prioritize areas that will make a tangible difference in your productivity, stress levels, and overall sense of peace.

Focus on the High-Impact Areas First

Some spaces you use daily have a greater impact on your mental and emotional well-being. Prioritize these spaces first. Take your home office, for example. If you spend most of your work hours there, but it's cluttered with unopened packages, papers you haven't filed, and general disorganization, every time you sit down to work, you will feel distracted and frustrated because of the mess. By tackling this space first, you'll immediately create a more productive and stress-free environment for yourself.

The kitchen, often the heart of your home, is often used multiple times a day for preparing meals, eating, and sometimes even socializing. A cluttered kitchen counter—filled with unused gadgets, dishes, and random items—can make the process of cooking feel like a chore rather than a joyful activity. Clearing the countertops and organizing the drawers can not only help you create more space but also make your time in the kitchen more enjoyable.

Consider How Often You Use the Space

If you work from home, your office or workspace might be your primary focus. For stay-at-home parents, the living room or play area may be more important. Consider how often you use each room and the time you spend there.

For example, if your bedroom is only used to sleep, as long as the bed is made, you may not notice the clutter in the corners or on your dresser. But if you work from home and use your bedroom as a quiet place to read or catch up on emails, the clutter in that space could have a bigger impact on your productivity and mental clarity. In this case, it might make sense to prioritize that space sooner rather than later.

The Flow of Your Day Matters

Think about the natural flow of your day.

- Where do you spend the most time?
- Which space frustrates you the most if it is disorganized?

Focusing on high-impact areas first can lead to quick wins that will keep you motivated throughout the decluttering process.

Take the bathroom, for instance. A bathroom cluttered with unused beauty products, old medications, and a jumble of towels, can become a source of stress each morning when you're trying to get ready. By decluttering this area, you'll feel more energized and organized, setting a positive tone for the rest of your day.

Use a Time vs. Impact Matrix

Simplify prioritization by using a Time vs. Impact matrix. Draw a simple chart with "Time" on one axis (how long it takes to declutter the area) and "Impact" on the other axis (how much of a difference decluttering that space will make in your life).

For example:

- **High time/high impact:** home office, kitchen, bedroom
- **Low time/high impact:** bathroom, entryway
- **Low time/low impact:** closet, guest room

This matrix quickly shows you where to focus your attention first. It's tempting to start with smaller, less impactful spaces just because they're easier to tackle. But the goal is to make the biggest difference in the shortest amount of time—prioritize the spaces that you use most and that will give you the highest return on your effort.

Consider Your Mental and Emotional Energy

Functionality matters, but consider how much mental energy certain rooms are costing you. A disorganized hallway or entryway signals a problem to your brain daily, even if you're not actively thinking about it (Sander, 2019). By organizing and decluttering this area, you remove that ongoing mental burden.

It's similar to the feeling you get when you open an overstuffed closet. You tell yourself you'll get to it eventually, but the clutter weighs on your subconscious, making you feel more stressed. Prioritizing these emotional triggers can significantly lighten your mental load.

Assessing Your Home's Current State Checklist

Use these checklists, as they can help you assess and prioritize your decluttering efforts effectively!

1. **I've walked through each room in my home with fresh eyes.**
2. True / False
3. **I've considered how each room functions for me and whether it supports my lifestyle.**
4. True / False
5. **I've evaluated how clutter in each room makes me feel emotionally.**
6. True / False
7. **I've identified specific emotional triggers caused by clutter in certain spaces.**
8. True / False
9. **I've checked hidden clutter in places like drawers, closets, and under the bed.**
10. True / False
11. **I've honestly assessed how often I use the items in these hidden clutter areas.**
12. True / False
13. **I've made a list of the spaces causing me the most stress.**
14. True / False
15. **I've prioritized the most frustrating rooms or areas based on urgency.**

16. True / False
17. **I've taken photos of cluttered areas to get a clearer perspective.**
18. True / False
19. **I've considered the functionality of my home and how each space supports my daily activities.**
20. True / False

Prioritizing Areas Based on Use and Impact Checklist

21. **I've identified which rooms or areas I use the most.**
22. True / False
23. **I've considered how much impact the clutter in each space has on my stress levels and productivity.**
24. True / False
25. **I've focused on spaces that will make the most difference in my daily routine.**
26. True / False
27. **I've started with high-impact areas, like the home office or kitchen, to improve productivity and well-being.**
28. True / False
29. **I've considered how often I use each room and how much clutter impacts me in those spaces.**
30. True / False
31. **I've thought about the natural flow of my day and which spaces will benefit the most from decluttering.**
32. True / False
33. **I've prioritized areas like the bathroom or entryway that have high impact but take less time to declutter.**
34. True / False
35. **I've used a Time vs. Impact matrix to help prioritize which areas to tackle first.**
36. True / False
37. **I've considered how much mental and emotional energy certain cluttered areas are costing me.**
38. True / False

39. **I've prioritized emotional triggers that create ongoing mental stress, like a disorganized hallway or overflowing closet.**
40. True / False

It's time to approach decluttering with structure. Rather than jumping in blindly and feeling overwhelmed, you can plan steps that align with your unique needs and goals. By having a clear roadmap, you'll stay focused, motivated, and empowered as you make progress.

Exercise: Set Clear, Specific Goals for Each Area

Decluttering an entire room can feel overwhelming, so break it down into manageable, specific goals. Instead of saying, "I'll declutter the living room," narrow it down. Focus on one aspect of the room at a time, perhaps the coffee table or the bookshelf. This not only makes the task more achievable but also lets you see progress quickly.

Here's how you can do it:

- **Write down specific goals:** List the rooms or areas you're prioritizing, then, set a clear goal for each. For example, in your kitchen, "Organize the pantry and clear off the countertops." For the bedroom, "Declutter the nightstand and under the bed."
- **Be specific:** A goal like "declutter my kitchen" is too broad. Instead, try, "Go through all the kitchen drawers and remove unused items," or "Sort through my spices and discard expired ones." The more specific, the better.
- **Set deadlines:** Assign a realistic timeline for each goal. For a specific space like your bedroom, decide whether you want to finish it in one session or break it into smaller tasks over the week.

The "Drop Zone" Organization

Creating a designated drop zone for frequently used items helps minimize clutter and makes it easier to maintain order.

Instructions

- Identify a clutter-prone area (entryway, kitchen counter, or living room table) where items tend to pile up.
- Set up a structured system using trays, bins, or hooks to store keys, mail, bags, or shoes.
- Assign a spot for every frequently used item and ensure everything is put back at the end of each day.
- Once a week, clear out any unnecessary buildup from the drop zone.

Identifying your goals, priorities, and timeline lays the foundation for a smoother, more enjoyable process. Remember, progress matters more than perfection. With your plan in place, tackle each area of your home with confidence, knowing that you have a roadmap to guide you through. Now, with a clear vision, it's time to focus on the heart of your home.

Next, we'll transform your living room into a peaceful sanctuary. It's the space where you relax, entertain, and gather with loved ones, so it is important that it reflects the calm, clarity, and joy you seek in your life. You'll learn a step-by-step approach to sorting through the items in your living room—from furniture to décor—ensuring that everything you keep serves a purpose and contributes to the overall harmony of the space.

3

DECLUTTERING THE LIVING ROOM—YOUR SANCTUARY AWAITS

P icture this: after a long day, you grab your favorite blanket, sink into the couch, and reach for the remote—but wait, where is it? You scan the room and find it buried under a pile of magazines, random toys, and yesterday's coffee mug. Instead of relaxing, you feel on edge, overwhelmed by the visual clutter in what should be your sanctuary.

The living room is often the space where you unwind, spend time with family, and entertain guests. But because it serves so many purposes, it's also one of the easiest spaces to become chaotic. From the remote that seems to migrate across the room to tangled cords by the TV, clutter here can quickly steal the peace you crave. The good news? With some simple strategies, you can transform your living room into a space that feels calm, functional, and inviting.

STRATEGIES FOR SORTING AND ORGANIZING COMMON AREAS

Your living room shouldn't be a catch-all for everything from last week's mail to spare blankets. Here's how to tackle this multifunctional space step by step.

Step 1: Divide and Conquer

Before you start organizing, access your living room and identify the categories of items that have accumulated. This clarifies what actually belongs in the space.

- **Sort by category:** Grab three large bins or baskets and label them "Keep," "Relocate," and "Donate/Trash." For example:
  - **Keep:** books, blankets, and family games that are used regularly
  - **Relocate:** items like socks, kids' homework, or kitchen utensils that don't belong here
  - **Donate/trash:** that decorative vase you never liked or the old magazines gathering dust
- **Tackle the surfaces first:** Start with the coffee table, side tables, and TV stand. Clear these areas before moving to shelves or drawers. For example, declutter the coffee table by removing everything except a few intentional items like a candle or a small stack of books.

Step 2: Create Functional Zones

Organizing your multipurpose living room into zones can help reduce clutter and increase functionality.

- **Relaxation zone:** This is where you spend most of your downtime. Ensure the seating area is clear and cozy. Keep only essential items here, like throw pillows and a blanket basket.
- **Entertainment zone:** Organize the TV area with storage solutions like baskets or bins for remotes, game controllers, and streaming devices. Consider a cord management system to keep wires hidden and tidy.
- **Play or activity zone (if applicable):** If your living room doubles as a space for kids or hobbies, designate a corner for toys, puzzles, or crafts. Use stackable bins or a storage ottoman to keep these items contained and out of sight.

For kids, invest in storage cubes with labels like "Legos" or "Art Supplies." This makes it easy for them to clean up and helps you maintain order.

Step 3: Use Storage Solutions Wisely

After sorting and creating zones, it's time to think about storage. Smart storage can make or break an organized living room.

- **Hidden storage:** Use furniture with built-in storage, like an ottoman that opens up for blankets or a coffee table with shelves underneath.
- **Vertical storage:** Maximize wall space by adding shelves for books or decorative items. Just make sure you don't overload them—a few well-placed accents create a more peaceful vibe.
- **Baskets and bins:** These are lifesavers for organizing loose items like remotes, toys, or pet supplies. For instance, place a decorative basket next to the couch to corral throw blankets or magazines.

Pro tip: Store items where you use them. Keep remotes in a tray on the coffee table, extra blankets in a basket near the couch, and board games on a shelf within reach.

Step 4: Minimize Visual Clutter

Even a clean living room can feel overwhelming if there's too much "visual noise." Here's how to keep things looking tidy:

- **Limit décor:** A gallery wall can be stylish, but too many knick-knacks or mismatched frames can create visual chaos. Stick to a few cohesive pieces.
- **Hide everyday essentials:** Use decorative boxes or lidded baskets to store things like TV remotes, chargers, or coasters. This keeps them accessible but out of sight.
- **Adopt a "One In, One Out" rule:** For every new item you bring into the living room—whether it's a throw pillow, candle, or piece of furniture—commit to removing something else. This prevents clutter from building up.

For example, if you buy a new decorative pillow for the couch, consider donating the one that no longer matches your aesthetic.

Step 5: Involve Your Household

Decluttering and organizing shouldn't be your sole responsibility, especially if you share the space with family members or roommates. Involve everyone in creating a system that works.

- **Set rules together:** Agree on guidelines like "No shoes in the living room" or "Toys must go back into bins after playtime."
- **Assign responsibilities:** If you live with others, assign specific tasks to keep the space tidy. For instance, one person can handle vacuuming while another is in charge of wiping down surfaces or organizing the shelves.
- **Lead by example:** If you consistently tidy up and stick to the system, others will follow your lead.

With your living room decluttered and organized, it's time to take your space from merely functional to truly inspiring. A well-organized living room should reflect your personal style and feel welcoming. This is where functionality meets aesthetics, and together, they transform a room into a space you'll love spending time in.

INCORPORATING FUNCTIONAL AND AESTHETIC ELEMENTS

Balancing function and beauty might seem like a challenge, but with a few intentional choices, your living room can serve both purposes seamlessly. Here's how to blend form and function effortlessly.

Anchor the Space With Multipurpose Furniture

Multipurpose furniture is the backbone of a living room that works hard while looking great.

- **Ottomans with hidden storage:** These are perfect for stashing away blankets, books, or even kids' toys while still providing a cozy place to rest your feet. Bonus: They can double as extra seating when guests are over.
- **Coffee tables with built-in storage:** Opt for a coffee table with drawers or a shelf underneath. Use decorative baskets on

the shelf to keep the look tidy while storing essentials like remotes or coasters.

- **Convertible furniture:** If your living room also functions as a guest room or office, consider a sleeper sofa or a foldable desk. These pieces allow you to switch up the space without sacrificing style.

For example, a friend transformed her living room into a multipurpose oasis by adding a sleek console table behind her sofa. It served as a charging station, an additional workspace, and a spot to display fresh flowers—all without taking up extra room.

Choose a Cohesive Color Palette

Your color scheme shapes both style and mood. Soft tones create calm while bold accents add energy.

- **Neutral foundations:** Start with neutral tones like beige, gray, or cream for your walls, furniture, and larger pieces. These create a versatile base that won't overwhelm the space.
- **Pop of personality:** Layer in pops of color through accessories like throw pillows, rugs, or wall art. For instance, if you love a cozy vibe, warm hues like rust or mustard can add depth without overpowering.
- **Tie it together:** Ensure your functional items match your aesthetic. If you're using baskets for storage, choose ones in natural materials, like wicker for a boho look or sleek metal for a modern vibe. One busy mom I know chose navy as her accent color because it hid the occasional spill from her toddler while still looking polished against her neutral couch and white walls.

Layer Lighting for Ambience

Lighting makes your living room both functional and inviting. Use a mix of light sources to create depth and adaptability.

- **Overhead lighting:** A statement chandelier or pendant light can provide ample light for the whole room while adding a focal point.
- **Task lighting:** Add floor lamps or table lamps near seating areas for reading or working. For example, a sleek arc lamp over a sectional can double as both a functional and aesthetic piece.
- **Ambient lighting:** Use string lights, candles, or dimmable bulbs to create a cozy atmosphere. This is especially useful in the evenings when you want to wind down.

Tip: If you're short on outlets, invest in rechargeable LED puck lights or smart bulbs. They're easy to install and allow you to control brightness and color with your phone.

Highlight Personal Touches

Personal touches make a space feel like home. These pieces should enhance the space without adding clutter.

- **Photos and art:** Frame your favorite family photos or choose artwork that inspires you. Stick to matching frames or a cohesive gallery wall layout for a polished look.
- **Books and collectibles:** Display a curated selection of books, travel souvenirs, or meaningful décor on open shelves. Use bookends or small trays to keep the arrangement tidy.
- **Greenery:** Add life to your living room with indoor plants. Even low-maintenance options like snake plants or pothos can make a big impact. If you lack a green thumb, faux plants are a great alternative.

A client turned her plain living room shelf into a conversation piece by arranging family heirlooms, her travel journal, and a few succulents in terracotta pots. The result? Personal yet uncluttered.

Focus on Comfortable Textures

Functionality is important, but your living room should be a place to unwind and relax. Incorporate layers of texture for a space that feels warm and cozy.

- **Throw pillows and blankets:** Use a mix of fabrics like velvet, cotton, or knits to add visual interest and comfort. Keep a basket nearby to store extras.
- **Area rugs:** Choose a rug that anchors the seating area and complements the color palette. A soft, plush rug adds warmth underfoot, while a patterned one can bring in some personality.
- **Curtains and upholstery:** Floor-to-ceiling curtains make a room feel taller, while upholstered furniture in durable fabrics ensures both style and practicality.

For example, one stay-at-home dad shared how his durable leather couch was a lifesaver with kids and pets, but he softened the look with a fluffy sheepskin throw and colorful pillows.

Maintain Flow With Thoughtful Layouts

Furniture placement can make or break the functionality of your living room. A well-planned layout ensures that the space feels open and easy to navigate.

- **Avoid overcrowding:** Leave enough space between furniture to allow for easy movement. A good rule of thumb is to aim for 18 inches between the coffee table and the couch.
- **Create conversation areas:** Arrange seating so people can easily chat without craning their necks. For example, place two armchairs opposite your couch with a side table in between.
- **Keep pathways clear**: If your living room connects to other rooms, ensure there's a clear walkway. Move any bulky furniture or décor that obstructs the natural flow.

Exercise 1: Mapping Out Zones for Purpose

Before rearranging furniture, it's essential to identify the primary functions of your living room. Whether it's a space for family movie nights, a spot to entertain guests, or a multi-purpose area that includes work or play, knowing how you use the space is key.

Instructions

1. **List your needs:** Write down everything you do in the living room. For example:
   ○ watching TV or movies
   ○ reading or working
   ○ playing with kids or pets
   ○ hosting guests
2. **Visualize activity zones:** Use masking tape to divide your living room floor into zones. For instance:
   ○ a cozy seating area near the TV
   ○ a reading nook by the window
   ○ a small play area for kids or pets in an unused corner
3. **Evaluate overlaps:** Look for ways to combine zones. For example, a coffee table can double as a play area during the day when cleared off, and the seating area can transition into a conversation space for guests.

Exercise 2: The "Paper Layout Test"

Redesigning a room can feel overwhelming, especially when moving heavy furniture. Save yourself the hassle (and backache) by trying this simple paper layout test before committing to a new arrangement.

Instructions:

1. **Measure your room and furniture:** Grab a tape measure and jot down the dimensions of your living room and each major piece of furniture.
2. **Create a scaled floor plan:** Draw a scaled version of your

living room on a large sheet of paper. Use graph paper for accuracy, with each square representing one foot.
3. **Cut out furniture templates:** Cut out paper shapes for each piece of furniture, matching their dimensions to the scale of your floor plan.
4. **Experiment with layouts:** Move the paper templates around to try different configurations. Consider:
    - positioning the sofa to face the main focal point (e.g., TV, fireplace, or window).
    - ensuring clear walkways, ideally at least three feet wide.
    - placing side tables and lamps within easy reach of seating.
5. **Choose your favorite:** Once you're happy with the paper layout, replicate it in real life.

Pro tip: Use free room design apps like Planner 5D or RoomSketcher if you prefer a digital approach.

Exercise 3: The "Live and Adjust" Trial Run

Sometimes, the best way to find the perfect layout is to test it out in real life and adjust it as needed. This exercise is particularly helpful for multi-purpose spaces or rooms with irregular layouts.

Instructions

1. **Start with the basics:** Arrange your largest furniture pieces first (e.g., sofa, coffee table, media console). Place them in positions that align with the primary purpose of the room.
2. **Add secondary pieces:** Bring in smaller items like side tables, armchairs, or bookcases. Keep the layout flexible so you can tweak things as needed.
3. **Test the flow:** Spend a week living in the new arrangement. Take note of what feels comfortable and what feels awkward. Pay attention to:
    - how easy it is to walk through the space.
    - whether the seating feels cozy and conversation-friendly.
    - any unused or overcrowded areas.

4. **Adjust as needed:** Don't be afraid to move things around until it feels just right. Sometimes, small tweaks, like angling a chair or shifting a table, can make a big difference.

Exercise 4: The "One Day Empty Room Challenge"

It's easy to get stuck in the same furniture arrangement just because that's how it's always been. This challenge allows you to see your living room with fresh eyes by temporarily clearing it out and reimagining its potential.

Instructions

1. **Remove as much as possible:** Take out all non-essential furniture and decor. If possible, temporarily move larger pieces to another room.
2. **Observe the empty space:** Notice how natural light enters, where traffic flows, and how open the room feels.
3. **Reintroduce items one by one:** Start with essential pieces like the sofa and primary seating, placing them where they feel most functional and aesthetically pleasing.
4. **Reevaluate each addition:** Before bringing an item back, ask:
   o Does this piece serve a purpose?
   o Is this the best location for it?
   o Could it be replaced with something better suited?
5. **Adjust and finalize:** Make small tweaks based on comfort and functionality once everything is back..

Emptying the room first will break old habits and create a fresh, intentional layout.

Exercise 5: The "Sightline Simplification" Test

Your living room should feel visually balanced, not cluttered or chaotic. This exercise helps identify distractions and unnecessary visual weight, creating a more harmonious space.

Instructions

1. **Take a photo of your living room:** Use your phone to snap a picture from different angles.
2. **Analyze the sightlines:** Look for areas that feel cluttered or unbalanced, such as:
   - too many small decor pieces in one area
   - large furniture blocking natural flow
   - mismatched colors disrupting visual cohesion
3. **Simplify focal points:** Remove or rearrange items to create a cleaner, more intentional arrangement if a particular area looks too busy.
4. **Apply the "rule of threes":** When styling shelves or tables, group items in odd numbers (e.g., three objects of varying heights).
5. **Repeat with fresh eyes:** After a day or two, revisit your space to see if it feels balanced.

This exercise helps refine your decor and layout by reducing visual clutter and emphasizing key focal points.

Exercise 6: The "Furniture on Wheels" Experiment

Flexibility is key for multifunctional spaces. This exercise introduces mobility by incorporating rolling furniture to adapt your living room layout as needed.

Instructions

1. **Identify moveable furniture:** Choose pieces like small tables, storage units, or ottomans that could benefit from added mobility.
2. **Add casters:** Attach rolling casters to selected items (many furniture stores sell easy-install options).

3. **Test different setups:** Experiment with moving pieces around throughout the day based on activities, such as:
   - rolling a coffee table closer for movie night
   - moving a side table near the sofa for work-from-home needs
   - shifting an ottoman for extra seating when guests arrive
4. **Evaluate convenience:** After a week, assess if mobility improved your space or if any refinements are needed.

This strategy makes your living room more adaptable to changing needs.

Exercise 7: The "Five Senses Atmosphere Check"

A well-designed living room isn't just about layout—it's about how the space makes you feel. This exercise ensures your space engages all five senses for a more comfortable, inviting environment.

Instructions

1. **Sight:** Assess lighting, colors, and decor. Does your living room feel too dark, overly bright, or visually cluttered? Adjust lighting and decor to create a balanced aesthetic.
2. **Sound:** Pay attention to the acoustics. Does the space echo or feel too noisy? Add soft textures like rugs, curtains, or cushions to absorb sound.
3. **Smell:** Identify any lingering odors. Use essential oils, scented candles, or fresh plants to introduce a pleasant aroma.
4. **Touch:** Sit on your furniture and feel different surfaces. Are they comfortable and inviting? Consider adding soft throws, textured pillows, or warmer materials.
5. **Taste (optional):** If you entertain often, create a small station for drinks or snacks that enhance the space, such as a coffee corner or a decorative fruit bowl.

By engaging all five senses, you'll create a more immersive and comfortable living space.

With your personalized plan in place, you're ready to transform the heart of your home: the living room. Next, we'll shift our focus to the kitchen, where another transformation awaits: making cooking easier and more enjoyable in a clutter-free zone.

4

TRANSFORMING THE KITCHEN— COOKING IN A CLUTTER- FREE ZONE

Have you ever opened a kitchen drawer only to be greeted by a tangled mess of utensils you barely use? Or spent precious minutes searching for that one elusive spatula buried under a pile of gadgets? The kitchen can quickly become a source of stress if it's overflowing with clutter. But what if your kitchen could be more than just a place to cook—a space that inspires creativity and makes every meal prep session feel effortless?

A clutter-free kitchen doesn't mean tossing everything out. It's about choosing the right tools, organizing with intention, and creating a space that works for you.

Let's jump into one of the most impactful steps: making your kitchen tools and utensils more efficient.

STREAMLINING KITCHEN TOOLS AND UTENSILS

The key to a functional, clutter-free kitchen starts with knowing what you truly need. Too often, we hold on to duplicates, rarely used gadgets, or impulse purchases that take up space without offering much value. Here's how to declutter and streamline your kitchen tools in a way that simplifies your daily routines.

Step 1: Empty and Assess

Start by pulling out all your kitchen tools and utensils from drawers, cabinets, and countertops. Yes, all of them! Seeing everything in one place helps you recognize just how much you own.

Ask Yourself

- How often do I use this?
- Is this tool still in good condition?
- Do I have duplicates that serve the same purpose?
- Does this item actually make my life easier?

You may discover that you own three vegetable peelers, but only one is sharp and comfortable to use. Or that garlic press you thought would be a time saver, but isn't. If you haven't touched it in months, it's time to let it go.

Step 2: Keep the Essentials

Once you've assessed everything, it's time to separate the must-haves from the unnecessary. Focus on tools that are versatile, durable, and genuinely useful in your day-to-day cooking.

Essentials to Keep

- a chef's knife and paring knife (well-maintained and sharp)
- a wooden spoon, spatula, and tongs
- a cutting board
- a can opener, vegetable peeler, and measuring cups/spoons
- a few high-quality pots and pans

Pro tip: Invest in multi-functional tools like a microplane (great for zesting, grating, and shredding) or a silicone spatula that can scrape, mix, and spread.

Step 3: Let Go of "Just in Case" Items

We all have those kitchen gadgets we keep around "just in case." Maybe it's the fondue set you used once at a holiday party or the avocado slicer that seemed genius in the store but is now collecting dust. Be honest—if it hasn't been used in the last year, it's probably not worth the space it's taking up.

A busy mom of two may realize that she hadn't touched her waffle maker in years because her kids preferred pancakes. Freeing up that shelf space will allow her to store her most-used blender within easy reach.

Step 4: Organize What You Keep

Now that you've narrowed down your collection, organize what's left to fit your workflow.

Tips for Organizing Kitchen Tools

- **Group by function:** Keep similar items together—spatulas and spoons in one drawer, knives in another.
- **Use dividers and trays:** Drawer dividers are perfect for preventing utensils from turning into a chaotic mess.
- **Prioritize accessibility:** Store frequently used items in the most accessible spots, like near the stove or prep area. Reserve

higher or harder-to-reach cabinets for seasonal or rarely used tools.

Pro tip: Hang tools like ladles, whisks, and measuring cups on hooks or a wall-mounted rack to free up drawer space and keep them within arm's reach.

Step 5: Limit Countertop Clutter

Your countertops should feel open and functional, not like an extra storage area. Only keep essentials like the coffee maker or toaster visible. Everything else should have a designated home in cabinets or drawers.

A chef can transform his counter by storing his knife block in a drawer and keeping cooking utensils in a sleek holder next to the stove. This simple change can create a clean and calming space and make cooking more enjoyable.

By streamlining your kitchen tools and utensils, you have freed up more valuable space. More importantly, you designed a kitchen that supports your cooking goals and helps you feel more in control. With fewer distractions and clutter, you'll find meal prep becomes quicker, easier, and even fun.

So, I think now you are ready to move on.

Let's tackle another vital area of the kitchen: your pantry and storage.

ORGANIZING THE PANTRY AND STORAGE EFFICIENTLY

Your pantry is more than just a storage space; it's the backbone of your kitchen. A well-organized pantry can save you time, reduce food waste, and make meal planning a breeze.

Here's how you can create a system that works for your busy life.

Step 1: Empty and Audit Your Pantry

Similarly to you did with your kitchen tools, start by removing everything from your pantry. This helps you to see exactly what you have and assess what needs to stay, what's expired, and what you'll never use.

What to Look For

- **Expired items:** Check dates on spices, canned goods, and dry foods. You'll be surprised how much can pile up.
- **Duplicates:** Do you really need five half-used bags of pasta? Consolidate where possible.
- **Forgotten ingredients:** That specialty flour you bought for one recipe three years ago, it's time to let it go.

For example, a friend realized she had ten jars of pasta sauce because she kept buying more, unaware of what was already hidden at the back of her pantry. After organizing, she now uses her stash without over-purchasing.

Step 2: Categorize and Group

Once your pantry is cleared, group similar items together. This makes items easier to find and creates a natural flow for restocking.

Categories to Consider

- grains and pasta
- canned goods
- baking supplies (flour, sugar, baking soda)
- snacks
- spices and condiments
- breakfast items (cereals, oatmeal, pancake mix)

Pro tip: Use clear containers for dry goods like rice, beans, and cereal. This keeps them fresh, but also lets you see exactly how much you have at a glance. Bonus: It looks tidy and Pinterest-worthy!

Step 3: Use the Right Storage Solutions

Good storage solutions can transform your pantry from cluttered to cohesive. Invest in tools that make your space functional and visually appealing.

Must-Have Storage Items

- **Stackable bins:** Perfect for grouping smaller items like snacks or baking ingredients.
- **Lazy susans:** Great for condiments, oils, or canned goods, so you can easily reach everything.
- **Clear containers:** Airtight containers are ideal for flour, sugar, and other pantry staples.
- **Tiered shelves:** These work wonders for canned goods or spices, ensuring nothing gets lost at the back.
- **Labels:** A simple label can make all the difference in maintaining your system.

A busy parent, for instance, can turn her chaotic pantry into an organized haven with labeled clear bins for her kids' snacks. This allows her kids to grab what they want without rummaging through shelves, and she has peace of mind knowing where everything is.

Step 4: Maximize Space With Creative Solutions

Not everyone has a walk-in pantry, but that doesn't mean you can't optimize the space you do have.

Ideas to Try

- **Door racks:** Use the back of your pantry door to hang spice racks, store condiments, or hold wraps and foil.
- **Under-shelf baskets:** These are perfect for small items like tea bags or extra napkins.
- **Pull-out baskets:** If your pantry shelves are deep, pull-out baskets let you access everything without a struggle.
- **Vertical dividers:** Store baking sheets, cutting boards, or serving trays upright to save space.

Pro tip: If you don't have a pantry, use a tall bookshelf or cabinets with added bins to mimic the same functionality.

Step 5: Create a Restocking System

An organized pantry is only as good as your ability to maintain it. Set up a simple system to keep it looking great.

Tips for Maintenance

- Rotate older items to the front so they get used first.
- Use a shopping list to prevent overbuying duplicates.
- Set a reminder every three months to do a quick inventory and clean-up.

For example, a chef keeps a small notepad on her pantry door to track items as they run out. This simple habit ensures she's never without her essentials and helps her stick to her grocery budget.

With your pantry organized, it's time to tackle an equally essential area: your refrigerator. A clutter-free fridge doesn't just make meal prep faster; it helps reduce food waste, saves money, and keeps your ingredients fresher for longer.

Let's look into simple ways to organize your refrigerator efficiently so that every time you open it, you're greeted with an oasis of order rather than chaos.

ORGANIZING YOUR REFRIGERATOR EFFICIENTLY

Your refrigerator is one of the hardest-working appliances in your home. From storing fresh produce to keeping leftovers safe, it's easy for things to get messy fast. But with a little planning and some smart techniques, you can transform it into a well-organized space that works for you, not against you.

Step 1: Empty, Clean, and Inspect

Before you start organizing, give your refrigerator a clean slate.

How to Get Started

1. **Empty it out:** Take everything out, placing perishables in a cooler or insulated bag to keep them safe while you work.
2. **Wipe it down:** Use a gentle, food-safe cleaner to scrub shelves, drawers, and walls.
3. **Inspect items:** Check for expired condiments, forgotten leftovers, and mystery items hiding in the back. Toss anything that's past its prime.

A friend discovered three bottles of mustard in her fridge after repeatedly buying more, thinking she was out. Clearing everything at once avoids these hidden duplicates and gives you a start fresh.

Step 2: Group Items by Category

Think of your refrigerator like a grocery store: everything has its designated section.

Key Categories to Consider

- **Dairy:** This includes milk, yogurt, cheese, and butter.
- **Meats and seafood:** Keep these on the bottom shelf or in a separate drawer to prevent cross-contamination.
- **Fruits and vegetables:** Store these in their designated crisper drawers for better freshness.
- **Leftovers:** Use a specific shelf for easy visibility.
- **Condiments:** Group them together on the door or in a bin.

Pro tip: Use clear bins inside your fridge to keep items like snacks, deli meats, or condiments contained and easy to grab.

Step 3: Optimize Shelf Placement

Not all parts of your refrigerator are created equal. Where you store items can impact how long they stay fresh.

Best Practices for Shelf Placement

- **Top shelves:** Great for ready-to-eat foods like leftovers, drinks, or prepped meals. This area is slightly warmer, so avoid storing anything highly perishable here.
- **Middle shelves:** Ideal for dairy products like eggs, milk, and cheese.
- **Bottom shelves:** Store raw meat and seafood here, as it's the coldest part of the fridge. It also reduces the risk of leaks contaminating other foods.
- **Crisper drawers:** Adjust the humidity settings—high for leafy greens and herbs, low for fruits like apples and citrus.

I recently reorganized my fridge using these rules, and it's been a game-changer. No more wilting lettuce or forgotten chicken tucked behind the yogurt. Everything has a home, and I know exactly where to find it.

Step 4: Use Labels for Easy Maintenance

Labels aren't limited to your pantry only. They can work wonders in your fridge, too.

How to Use Labels Effectively

- Label shelves or bins with categories like "Snacks," "Leftovers," or "Deli Items."
- Use dry-erase markers on containers for a temporary, flexible solution.
- Label leftovers with the date they were made to avoid keeping them too long.

Pro tip: A busy chef I know labels her kids' snack bins in the fridge. It keeps them from rummaging through everything, and she never has to wonder what's running low.

Step 5: First In, First Out (FIFO)

Adopt the grocery store method of "first in, first out" to reduce waste and keep your fridge organized.

How to Implement FIFO

- Rotate older items to the front so they get used before newer ones.
- When putting away groceries, place the freshest items in the back.
- Use a small bin labeled "Eat Me First" for perishables nearing their expiration date.

A stay-at-home parent I know used to toss out nearly $50 worth of spoiled produce every month—until this simple habit changed that. Now, she rarely throws food away.

Step 6: Maximize Door Storage Strategically

The refrigerator door is the warmest spot in your fridge, so be mindful of what you store there.

What Works Best in the Door

- **Condiments** such as ketchup, mustard, and salad dressings.
- **Beverages** like juices, sodas, and non-dairy milk.
- **Butter and soft cheeses** as these can handle slightly warmer temperatures.

Avoid storing these here: Eggs and milk are better off in the colder sections of your fridge to stay fresh longer.

Step 7: Maintain a Weekly Reset Routine

Even the most organized refrigerator needs regular upkeep to stay that way.

Your Weekly Routine

1. Do a quick inventory before grocery shopping.
2. Wipe down any spills or crumbs.
3. Toss out anything that's expired or is unlikely to be used.
4. Restock using the same system.

Judy, a busy graphic designer, sets aside 10 minutes every Sunday to tidy her fridge. It's her secret to keeping it functional and avoiding midweek meal prep frustration.

Practical Exercises: Creating a Meal Prep-Friendly Kitchen

Set Up a Meal Prep Station

Having a dedicated meal prep zone simplifies the process and minimizes chaos.

Instructions

- Identify a section of your countertop near key appliances, like the stove, oven, or sink.
- Organize this area with the tools you use most often for meal prep, such as a cutting board, knives, measuring cups, and mixing bowls.
- Add a container or small drawer organizer for quick access to smaller essentials like vegetable peelers, can openers, and garlic presses.

Pro tip: Use a large cutting board with a built-in groove to catch juices or crumbs. It keeps your counter tidy and reduces cleanup time.

Create a Weekly Ingredient Prep Routine

Make your kitchen meal prep ready by prepping common ingredients in advance.

Instructions

- Pick a day (Sunday works great for most) to wash, chop, and portion your ingredients.
- Store chopped veggies, like carrots, bell peppers, and celery, in clear containers in the fridge.
- Pre-cook staples like rice, quinoa, or roasted chicken and store them in airtight containers for easy grab-and-go meals.

Pro tip: Use masking tape and a marker to label containers with the prep date, ensuring you use items while they're fresh.

Stock Meal Prep Containers Wisely

The right containers can make or break your meal prep efforts.

Instructions

- Invest in a variety of stackable, airtight containers in different sizes. Look for glass or BPA-free plastic options.

- Keep lids organized by size, or use a lid organizer to avoid the dreaded "Where's the lid?" scramble.
- Include smaller containers for dressings, sauces, and snacks to keep portions tidy.

Pro tip: Label containers with the meal type (e.g., "Monday Lunch") to save time when grabbing food on busy days.

Incorporate Meal Prep-Friendly Gadgets

Certain tools can speed up your prep time and reduce the effort required to prepare meals.

Instructions

- Consider gadgets like a food processor, mandolin slicer, or an Instant Pot to streamline your cooking.
- Dedicate a shelf or cabinet to these meal prep tools, so they're easy to grab when needed.
- Avoid overcrowding by limiting gadgets to those you genuinely use regularly.

Pro tip: If you're short on counter space, look for multi-functional tools like a blender that doubles as a food processor.

With your living room and kitchen feeling more functional, now it's time to focus on the space where your rest and relaxation happen: the bedroom. Decluttering your wardrobe and closet can make a huge difference in how you feel when you enter your room. In the upcoming chapter, we will discuss creating a calming and restorative environment that helps promote better sleep. You'll feel rejuvenated just walking into your newly organized bedroom.

5

MASTERING THE BEDROOM— RESTFUL RETREATS BEGIN HERE

Have you ever walked into your bedroom after a long day only to feel overwhelmed by the clutter and chaos surrounding you? When your sanctuary has become a storage unit, relaxation turns into stress. I know exactly how it feels. My friend once told me how every morning she would shove piles of clothes off her bed just to make space to sit down. She couldn't understand why she never felt fully rested, even though she had a nice bed, soft pillows, and cozy sheets. It wasn't until she started organizing her bedroom did she realize how much clutter was impacting her peace of mind.

The bedroom should be your retreat, a place to rest, recharge, and rejuvenate. But it's easy to let things pile up—clothes on the floor and random items on every surface. It's time to reclaim that space and transform it into the restful retreat you deserve.

So, let's take a closer look!

Simplifying Wardrobe and Closet Organization

Simplifying your wardrobe and closet is one of the most effective ways to do that. Think about how often you've rifled through clothes, trying to find that one shirt or those comfy jeans, only to feel frustrated by the mess. A tidy, well-organized closet not only saves time but also reduces stress, allowing you to start your day on a positive note.

Take Everything Out and Start Fresh

It's hard to visualize an organized space if you're staring at the clutter. Start by emptying your closet completely. Yes, every single item—clothes, shoes, bags, and accessories. This step may feel overwhelming, but trust me—seeing everything laid out makes it much easier to make decisions about what to keep and what to let go of.

How to Do It

- Lay everything out on your bed or a large surface.
- Take a few minutes to breathe and get in the mindset that this process is about clearing the clutter for a calmer, more organized space.

- Go through each item and ask yourself: *Have I worn this in the past year? Does it fit? Is it in good condition? Does it make me feel good when I wear it?*

Pro tip: If you're struggling to decide, try the "hanger trick." Hang all your clothes with the hangers facing the opposite direction. After you wear something, turn the hanger around. In a few months, you'll be able to see clearly what you haven't worn and what can be donated.

A friend of mine, a teacher who is always on the go, recently did a closet clean-out. She was amazed at how many clothes still had tags on them, taking up space. It was a huge relief when she was able to donate several bags of clothes she never wore.

Categorize and Sort Your Clothes

Once you've decided what stays, it's time to categorize your wardrobe. Organizing your closet by type will help you save time every morning and avoid the endless digging through piles of clothes.

How to Do It

- Start by grouping items into categories: dresses, shirts, pants, outerwear, shoes, and accessories.
- If you have a lot of similar items, consider subcategorizing by color, season, or fabric type.
- Fold or hang clothes in a way that makes it easy to see everything at a glance. For example, keep all your work clothes in one section and casual clothes in another.

Pro tip: Use slim, non-slip hangers for tops and dresses to maximize hanging space. For pants, you can use multi-bar hangers to save room to prevent wrinkles.

A client I worked with had a habit of throwing her workout clothes into a random pile. After she had reorganized them by type and frequency of use—keeping her yoga pants and sports bras within easy reach—she found herself getting dressed more quickly and actually enjoying her workouts more.

Invest in Storage Solutions That Fit Your Needs

Not all closets are created equal. You may need a few extra tools to truly optimize your space. Invest in smart storage solutions that work for your particular needs.

How to Do It

- Consider shelf dividers for sweaters, jeans, or shoes to keep everything neatly in place.
- Add clear bins or baskets for accessories like scarves, hats, or belts.
- Use under-bed storage for seasonal items, like winter coats or summer clothes, to keep your closet from becoming overcrowded.

Pro tip: Label bins or baskets to easily identify contents, especially for smaller items like handbags or scarves. Clear containers work best for this, as they allow you to view what's inside at a glance.

A busy friend of mine started using hanging organizers for shoes in her closet. She used to struggle with shoe clutter, but now she can easily see and grab a pair of shoes without wasting time looking through piles.

Create a Maintenance Routine

An organized closet doesn't stay that way on its own—it requires regular maintenance. By dedicating just a few minutes each week to keeping things neat, you can avoid the dreaded closet chaos from building up again.

How to Do It

- Spend five minutes every week going through your closet to put items back where they belong.

- If you buy something new, donate or discard an old item to keep your wardrobe manageable.
- Once a season, go through your clothes to ensure that everything still fits and is in good condition.

Pro tip: Consider a 30-day "one in, one out" rule: for every new item you buy, commit to donating or getting rid of something old. This will keep your closet from becoming overcrowded.

A busy stay-at-home mom I worked with set a reminder on her phone to declutter her closet once a week. It only takes her about 10 minutes to keep things organized, and she's noticed it makes a big difference in her overall peace of mind.

DESIGNING A CALMING AND RESTORATIVE ENVIRONMENT

Now that you've simplified your wardrobe and created an organized space, it's time to elevate your bedroom to the next level by transforming it into a calming and restorative environment. Think of your bedroom as a retreat where you can recharge and rest—physically, mentally, and emotionally. A well-organized space contributes to relaxation, but it's the atmosphere you cultivate that truly enhances your sense of calm and tranquility.

Set the Mood With Color

Color has a strong influence on your mood and energy levels. Choosing the right colors in your bedroom can enhance relaxation, improve sleep quality, and even help reduce stress. While bold and vibrant colors might energize you, soft and muted tones can encourage relaxation. A friend of mine switched her bedroom from bright, bold colors to soft grays and calming blues. She shared that it felt like an instant transformation, and she found it helped her unwind more easily at the end of each day.

How to Do It

- Stick with soft neutrals, pastels, or earthy tones like light blues, soft grays, sage greens, or warm beiges. These colors are known for their calming effects and can help create a peaceful atmosphere (Space Refinery, 2024).
- If you love a particular accent color, use it sparingly in accessories like throw pillows, rugs, or art. This way, the space remains soothing without feeling over-stimulating.
- Think about the psychology of color—blue is calming, green symbolizes growth and renewal, and beige creates warmth and coziness.

Pro tip: If painting your room isn't an option, opt for soft, calming colors in your bed linens, curtains, and wall art. You don't have to repaint your whole space to make a difference!

Incorporate Natural Elements

Emma had always struggled with restless nights. Between the hum of the city outside her window and the never-ending stream of notifications from her phone, true relaxation felt impossible. That was until she discovered the power of nature in her own bedroom. One weekend, she set out to transform her space. First, she visited a local plant nursery and picked up a few low-maintenance greens: a snake plant for the corner by her bed, a peace lily near the window, and a collection of tiny succulents for her nightstand. As she arranged them, she instantly felt a shift in the energy of the room. Next, she swapped her synthetic bedding for soft, breathable linen sheets. The natural fabric felt cool and comforting against her skin, a small but noticeable difference. She also replaced her heavy, artificial-fiber curtains with flowing cotton ones, which allowed the morning sunlight to filter through gently.

Wanting to take things a step further, Emma added a small tabletop fountain on her dresser. The quiet trickling of water had an almost hypnotic effect, making her feel as if she were beside a bubbling stream rather than in the middle of a bustling city. That night, for the first time in what felt like forever, Emma slept soundly. The air in her room felt fresher, her mind calmer. As she was sleeping, surrounded by the gentle presence of nature, she realized something profound: sometimes, the simplest changes could make the biggest difference.

Nature has an incredible way of promoting peace and reducing stress. Adding natural elements to your bedroom can create grounding, harmony, and rejuvenation (Song et al., 2023). Whether it's through plants, natural fibers, or outdoor-inspired décor, you can achieve a serene, nature-infused atmosphere.

How to Do It

- Bring in a few low-maintenance indoor plants like snake plants, peace lilies, or succulents. Not only do they add a pop of green, but they also purify the air, which can improve your sleep quality (Song et al., 2023).
- Use natural materials like cotton, linen, or wool for bedding, curtains, and rugs. These fabrics feel more breathable and connected to nature.
- Consider adding a small water feature like a tabletop fountain for the soothing sound of flowing water that can promote relaxation.

Pro tip: Be mindful of the placement of plants. Put them near natural light, but avoid overcrowding the space, as too many plants can make the room feel chaotic.

Optimize Lighting for Relaxation

Lighting is essential in creating a calming bedroom environment. Bright overhead lights can be jarring, while soft, layered lighting eases tension and prepares you for restful sleep. The right lighting sets the mood and enhances the overall ambience of the room.

Lisa had always struggled with winding down at the end of the day. As a stay-at-home parent, her days were hectic: making breakfast, packing lunches, tidying up endless messes, and ensuring her two young children were happy and well cared for. By the time evening arrived, her body was exhausted, but her mind refused to slow down. The harsh glare of the overhead ceiling light in her bedroom only seemed to make things worse.

One evening, after yet another restless night, she decided to make a small change. She purchased two dimmable lamps and placed one on each side of the bed. She also swapped out the bright, cool-toned bulbs in her ceiling fixture for softer, warmer ones. She had read somewhere that lighting played a big role in relaxation, and though she wasn't sure it would make much of a difference, she was willing to try anything.

That night, after putting the kids to bed, Lisa switched on the dimmable lamp next to her and turned off the overhead light. A warm, golden glow filled the room. She picked up a book she had been meaning to read for months and sank into her pillows. To her surprise, the usual tension in her shoulders melted away. She wasn't instantly sleepy, but she felt calmer, more at peace.

Over the next few weeks, Lisa's new lighting routine became a ritual. She no longer scrolled endlessly on her phone before bed. Instead, she let the soft light guide her into relaxation, and before she knew it, she was falling asleep faster and waking up feeling more rested. It was a simple change, but for Lisa, it made all the difference.

How to Do It

- Use warm light bulbs in your lamps instead of harsh, bright white ones. Soft white or amber-colored lighting promotes relaxation and better sleep (Yetman, 2024).
- Invest in dimmable lamps or light fixtures so you can adjust the intensity depending on the time of day and your mood.
- Incorporate accent lighting like fairy lights, floor lamps, or even candles for a cozy and intimate atmosphere. Avoid any flickering or overly bright light sources.

Pro tip: Try using smart bulbs or a light timer so you can set the lighting to automatically dim or brighten based on the time of day.

Enhance Sleep With the Right Bedding

The quality of your bed and bedding directly impacts your relaxation and sleep quality. A clean, well-made bed can be a powerful tool in signaling to your body that it's time to unwind.

How to Do It

- Invest in comfortable, breathable sheets, pillows, and blankets. High-quality cotton or linen sheets will feel soft and cozy, enhancing comfort.
- Choose pillows that support your sleeping style. Whether you sleep on your side, back, or stomach, make sure your pillow provides proper alignment for your neck.
- Don't skimp on the mattress—if it's time for a new one, select one that aligns with your personal comfort preferences.

Pro tip: Keep your bedding fresh by washing your sheets weekly and fluffing your pillows regularly. A clean, inviting bed greatly enhances a restorative environment.

Declutter for Calm

Decluttering your space means tidying up and creating a sense of peace. A cluttered room can cause mental clutter, leading to stress and difficulty relaxing. Keeping only the essentials in your bedroom helps to promote clarity and calm.

A work-from-home client found it helpful to set a rule that no work-related items were allowed in her bedroom. This simple change made her bedroom feel more like a true retreat rather than just another office space.

How to Do It

- Keep surfaces like nightstands and dressers clear of unnecessary items. Leave only things that serve a function or bring you comfort, like a lamp or a good book.

- Use storage solutions like baskets, shelves, or bins to store items out of sight. Having everything in its place reduces visual clutter and contributes to a more peaceful environment.
- Limit electronics in your bedroom. Instead of watching TV or scrolling through your phone, create a routine that encourages relaxation, like reading or journaling.

Pro tip: Make a habit of tidying up before bed. Even a quick five-minute tidy-up can make a big difference in how calm and restful your room feels.

Practical Exercises for Implementing the Capsule Wardrobe Concept

With your bedroom now a calming retreat, it's time to focus on making your wardrobe a source of simplicity, ease, and intentionality. A key step is adopting the **Capsule Wardrobe Concept**. By curating a collection of versatile, timeless pieces that complement each other, you can streamline your closet—saving time, reducing decision fatigue, and giving you more space to breathe.

This concept is all about minimalism and quality over quantity. Instead of filling your closet with trendy items you rarely wear, a capsule wardrobe allows you to focus on the essentials (Sethi, 2024). Think of it as curating a wardrobe that speaks to your personal style, meets your daily needs, and, most importantly, keeps your space organized.

Take Stock: Start With a Closet Cleanse

Before building your capsule wardrobe, you need to assess what you already own. This step is crucial. It's about identifying what works, what doesn't, and what's just taking up space.

How to Do It

- Take everything out of your closet. Yes, everything! Lay it all out on your bed or in your living room.

- Go through each item one by one and ask yourself: *Does this piece fit me well? Is it something I actually wear? Does it fit my lifestyle and personal style?*
- Sort items into three piles: **Keep**, **Donate/Sell**, and **Maybe**. The "Maybe" pile should be revisited later, and you can do this after some time has passed to make sure you're being objective.
- If you haven't worn something in the past year, let it go. This step helps create clarity and prevents emotional attachments from clouding your judgment.

One client found that after completing this cleanse, she had more space to breathe and less decision fatigue when getting dressed in the morning. It was a game-changer for her productivity and mental clarity.

Identify Your Core Style

The next step is understanding your style preferences—what makes you feel confident and comfortable. A capsule wardrobe works best when it's aligned with who you are and what makes you feel good.

How to Do It

- Take a moment to reflect on your lifestyle, needs, and values.
  - Do you need professional attire for work?
  - Do you prefer athleisure for comfort?
  - Do you have a special leaning toward a more minimalist look or love statement pieces?
- Create a Pinterest board or look through fashion magazines to pin styles that speak to you. As you collect images, look for common themes.
  - Do you favor neutral tones?
  - Do you want structured silhouettes?
  - Do you crave simple and clean designs?
- Consider the colors and textures that make you feel most at

ease. This will help you focus on pieces that are easy to mix and match.

For example, you can embrace a capsule wardrobe only to note that the simpler and more neutral the tones, the easier it is to mix and match, creating multiple outfits from just a few items.

Choose Your Color Palette

A cohesive color palette is a cornerstone of a capsule wardrobe. By sticking to a specific range of colors, you'll ensure that everything in your closet can be easily paired together, creating a multitude of outfit combinations.

How to Do It

- Choose a primary color (like navy, black, or beige) that serves as the foundation for your wardrobe.
- Add one or two accent colors that can be used in smaller quantities (think scarves, accessories, or shoes). These colors should complement your primary color but provide variety and interest.
- Stick to neutral tones for the majority of your pieces—these tend to be timeless and versatile, making them perfect for layering or dressing up/down.

A professional who worked from home embraced a monochrome color scheme of navy and gray, which gave her flexibility while still maintaining a sharp, professional appearance.

Evaluate Quality vs. Quantity

One of the hallmarks of a capsule wardrobe is selecting pieces that are of high quality, durable, and versatile. Think about clothing that will last and withstand wear.

How to Do It

- As you go through your items, evaluate the quality of each piece.
    - Does it hold up after several washes?
    - Is it made of natural fabrics like cotton, wool, or linen, which tend to last longer than synthetic ones?
- Consider your clothing's versatility. Does it pair well with multiple outfits? Is it suitable for different occasions (work, weekends, dinner out, etc.)?
- Instead of buying trendy pieces that will likely go out of style, focus on investment items that you can wear for years to come.

A friend of mine opted for a few high-quality jackets that could be styled differently for both casual and business settings. They lasted much longer than cheaper alternatives and provided more variety than expected.

Create a Functional "Outfit Formula"

Capsule wardrobes thrive on simplicity. Creating outfit formulas and basic guidelines that make putting together an outfit easier allows you to maximize your wardrobe's potential with minimal effort.

How to Do It

- Choose staple pieces (e.g., a neutral blouse, black pants, denim jacket, and simple accessories) that can be combined in different ways.
- Create three to five go-to outfit combinations for everyday wear. For example:
    - Button-up shirt + jeans + flats = casual but put-together look
    - Blazer + black trousers + loafers = work-ready chic
    - Sweater + leggings + ankle boots = weekend cozy

- Rotate your core items to keep things fresh without feeling overwhelmed by choice.

A stay-at-home mom who needed to juggle errands, meetings, and kids' activities found that adopting an outfit formula saved her time. She no longer spent time figuring out what to wear each morning.

Invest in Multi-Purpose Pieces

Versatility is key in a capsule wardrobe. The goal is to minimize the number of clothes while maximizing their functionality.

How to Do It

- Look for pieces that can serve multiple purposes. For instance, a blazer can work for a business meeting, a night out, or even dressed down with jeans for a casual look.
- Opt for clothing that can transition from one season to the next with just a few adjustments. A lightweight sweater, for example, can be worn with layers in the winter or on its own in the warmer months.
- Shoes can also play a big role in versatility. A pair of ankle boots can work with dresses, skirts, or jeans, serving multiple looks.

Set a Clothing Budget and Stick to It

Capsule wardrobes are about intentional purchasing. Instead of buying clothing on impulse, set a budget that aligns with your priorities and stick to it.

How to Do It

- Calculate your clothing budget by considering your lifestyle and current needs. Avoid overbuying and focus on replacing items only when necessary.
- Plan your purchases carefully. Stick to your core colors and

styles, and avoid impulse buys that don't contribute to your overall wardrobe strategy.

- Reevaluate your wardrobe every season to see what's been worn regularly and what hasn't. This way, you stay aligned with the idea of quality over quantity.

One client, Nora, always struggled with overspending on clothes. She loved fashion but often made impulsive purchases, buying trendy items that she rarely wore or snagging sale pieces just because they were discounted. Her closet was overflowing, yet she constantly felt like she had nothing to wear.

When she decided to create a capsule wardrobe, the first step was setting a realistic budget. She calculated how much she could comfortably spend without straining her finances and committed to only buying pieces that truly added value to her wardrobe. Instead of mindlessly shopping, she planned her purchases carefully, sticking to neutral colors, timeless styles, and high-quality fabrics that would last.

Within a few months, Nora noticed a considerable difference. Not only was her closet more organized and functional, but she also felt more in control of her spending. She no longer experienced buyer's remorse, and her financial stress eased because she knew exactly where her money was going. "For the first time, I feel like I'm buying clothes that work *for* me, rather than just collecting things," she shared. By aligning her budget with her needs, she transformed both her wardrobe and her relationship with money.

Now that your bedroom is a calming haven, it's time to set up a workspace that boosts your productivity and keeps distractions at bay. The next chapter looks at organizing your home office for maximum efficiency. You'll also explore the importance of digital decluttering to keep your files and devices organized. Whether you work from home full-time or just need a designated space for focused work, you'll see how to set up a workspace that works for you.

6

STREAMLINING THE HOME OFFICE—BOOSTING PRODUCTIVITY

You know that feeling when you sit down at your desk, only to be instantly overwhelmed by the clutter and chaos surrounding you? You try to focus, but your eyes keep darting to the pile of papers in the corner, the stack of books you've been meaning to read, or the sticky notes covering your computer screen. It's hard to feel productive when your workspace constantly reminds you of unfinished tasks.

Then, you decide to take control. You clear the clutter, reorganize your desk, and suddenly, the fog starts to lift. You've created a space that's designed for focus and productivity, and the difference it makes is immediate. Tasks that once felt overwhelming now seem more manageable, and you begin to realize how much your environment influences your ability to get things done.

That's the power of a streamlined home office. Your environment plays a huge role in your productivity, and when you take the time to organize your workspace effectively, you unlock your true potential.

Now, let's learn how to work on boosting productivity.

Organization is essential in creating an efficient workspace. Whether you're working from home full-time, managing a side hustle, or juggling multiple tasks as a stay-at-home parent, your workspace needs to serve you, not the other way around.

Follow these practical steps to help you optimize your workspace, increase efficiency, and foster a productive mindset.

Declutter and Simplify

The first step to an organized workspace is decluttering. It's easy for papers, office supplies, and miscellaneous items to pile up over time. But the more cluttered your desk becomes, the harder it is to stay focused.

Instructions

- Start by taking everything off your desk. Yes, everything. Papers, pens, gadgets, and décor.
- Sort through the items. Keep only what you use regularly, and what's essential for your work. If something doesn't serve a purpose, let it go.
- Invest in storage solutions, like drawer organizers or file holders, to keep important documents neatly tucked away. Consider using a digital filing system to go paperless.

A freelance writer I know found that clearing her desk of everything except her laptop and a cup of pens helped her concentrate more. She also discovered she worked faster, with fewer distractions, and felt more accomplished at the end of the day.

Optimize Your Desk Layout

How you arrange the items on your desk can have a huge impact on how efficiently you work. The goal is to make sure everything you need is within reach but not overwhelming.

Instructions

- Keep your desk surface clean and clear. Use trays or organizers for pens, notebooks, and other frequently used items.
- Position your computer or workspace tools to minimize strain on your body. For example, your monitor should be at eye level to prevent neck strain, and your keyboard and mouse should be positioned comfortably to avoid wrist pain.
- If space is limited, consider vertical storage options like floating shelves or pegboards to keep your desk area tidy while still having access to all your essentials.

One business partner I worked with found that moving her printer to the other side of the room and placing her laptop in the center of her desk, improved her workflow dramatically. She no longer felt cramped, and the open space around her allowed her to think more clearly.

Designate Zones for Specific Tasks

Creating designated zones for different tasks can help you stay organized and focused. If your workspace is multifunctional, such as a home office that doubles as a creative studio or a place for *Zoom* calls —organizing these spaces can improve how you work.

Instructions

- Designate a specific area for your computer work, another for writing or note-taking, and perhaps a separate area for brainstorming or phone calls.
- If you're working on a particular project, set aside a dedicated space for all related materials (laptop, research papers, or even your whiteboard).
- Use visual cues like baskets, labels, or color-coded items to keep these areas organized and easy to access.

A designer friend found that separating her desk into clear zones for sketching, digital design, and project management helped her stay focused. Instead of constantly shifting between tasks and materials, she could seamlessly transition between different areas of work.

Use Technology to Your Advantage

Technology is your friend when it comes to organizing your workspace. Project management apps, time trackers, and other digital tools help you stay organized and on track.

Instructions

- Use a task management app (like *Trello*, *Asana*, or *Notion*) to keep track of your to-dos and deadlines.
- Set up a digital filing system that allows you to easily find and organize your documents. Cloud storage services like *Google Drive* or *Dropbox* are great for keeping everything in one place.
- Consider using a focus timer or time-blocking method (like the Pomodoro Technique) to stay productive throughout the day.

A busy stay-at-home parent used *Trello* to manage family schedules and work tasks, while *Google Drive* kept all her documents neatly organized. She realized that digital organization was just as important as the physical setup in helping her stay productive and on top of her day.

Prioritize Ergonomics and Comfort

A clutter-free workspace is important, but so is comfort. If you're spending hours at your desk, you need a workspace that promotes both physical and mental well-being.

Instructions

- Invest in an ergonomic chair that supports your back and promotes good posture.
- Make sure your desk is at the right height for your body, and use a keyboard and mouse that reduce strain on your wrists.
- Keep items like a comfortable lamp or plants nearby to create a space that's visually pleasing and energizing.

DIGITAL DECLUTTERING: MANAGING FILES AND DEVICES

Having streamlined your physical workspace and optimized your home office for maximum productivity, it's time to tackle the digital clutter. Like most people, you've probably accumulated an excessive number of files, emails, photos, and documents across your devices.

It's easy to let your digital life become overwhelming. Whether it's an overflowing email inbox, hundreds of unorganized files on your desktop, or a phone filled with outdated apps and photos, digital clutter can feel just as draining as physical clutter. The good news is that, just like decluttering your home, digital decluttering is entirely within your control, and the payoff can be huge.

Clearing digital clutter will free up space but also create a smoother and more efficient workflow, allowing you to focus on what truly matters.

Let's look into how you can manage your files and devices more effectively to boost your productivity and mental clarity.

Clean Up Your Desktop and Files

Your computer desktop is often the first place where files accumulate. But over time, this can lead to a disorganized mess that actually slows you down.

Instructions

- Start by clearing everything off your desktop. It can feel daunting at first, but you'll be surprised at how much more efficiently you can work when your desktop is clean and free of distractions.
- Create folders that logically group files together. For example, if you're a freelance writer, you can create folders for "Clients," "Projects," and "Research." Keep the number of folders manageable and simple to avoid creating more chaos.
- Move files that you don't need immediate access to into cloud storage or an external drive. *Google Drive, Dropbox, or OneDrive are* great for keeping things accessible without cluttering your physical storage.

A small business owner I worked with had a desktop full of random images, documents, and receipts. Spending just 30 minutes to organizing her files into folders and deleting duplicates saved her time but reduced her stress levels, too.

Sort and Organize Your Email Inbox

An overflowing inbox can be just as overwhelming as a messy desk. With promotional emails, personal messages, and work-related tasks, it's easy to lose track of important messages.

Instructions

- Use labels, folders, or categories to organize your inbox into manageable sections. For instance, you might set up folders for "Work," "Personal," "Receipts," or "Newsletters."
- Unsubscribe from emails that you no longer need. Apps like *Unroll.Me* make this process faster and easier.
- Set aside specific times during the day to check your email to prevent it from becoming a distraction. The less time you spend sifting through emails, the more time you'll have to focus on the tasks that matter.

A friend of mine who works from home found that unsubscribing from all those online store emails eliminated daily distractions. It gave her back time to focus on more important work.

Tidy Up Your Phone and Apps

Our phones can quickly become digital junk drawers filled with apps, photos, and files that we rarely use. Just like your computer, your phone benefits from a regular decluttering session.

Instructions

- Delete or archive old apps that you no longer use. This will free up space and simplify your phone's interface.
- Organize your apps into folders by category (e.g., "Productivity," "Social," "Health," etc.) so that you can find them more easily.
- Back up important photos and documents to a cloud service (Google Photos, iCloud) and delete any duplicates or blurry photos. You'll be amazed at how much space this frees up.

Organize Your Digital Files Across Devices

If you work on multiple devices, it's easy for files to get scattered across your laptop, tablet, and phone. This makes it harder to find what you need when you can't remember where you saved it.

Instructions

- Use cloud storage services to keep important documents in one place. Syncing your devices ensures you can access your files, no matter where you are, without the hassle of searching through multiple locations.
- Set a file naming convention that works for you, such as "Year-Month-Day_ProjectName." This makes it easier to locate specific files when you need them.
- Periodically review your files and delete or archive anything that's outdated or no longer necessary.

For example, a busy professional juggling several projects found that using *Google Drive* to sync his work between his laptop and phone saved him hours of searching through multiple folders. He began naming files by date and project, which made organizing and retrieving them a breeze.

Maintain Digital Minimalism

Digital clutter isn't limited to files. It also comes from constant notifications, apps, and digital distractions that demand your attention. Adopting a minimalist approach to your digital life can help you stay focused and present.

Instructions

- Turn off non-essential notifications on your devices to minimize distractions. Only keep notifications for things that directly affect your productivity.
- Declutter your digital life by simplifying your apps and tools. Do you really need all the apps on your phone? Could you

consolidate multiple tools into one? Consider merging your task manager, calendar, and notes into one app to simplify things.

- Streamline your social media. Unfollow accounts that no longer serve you and turn off notifications for platforms that drain your energy.

Backup and Archive Important Information

It's easy to forget about backup and archiving, but having a system in place for protecting your important files is crucial for peace of mind.

Instructions

- Set up automatic backups for your important files using cloud services like *Google Drive* or *iCloud*, or an external hard drive.
- Periodically review your backup system to ensure that everything important is included and that old files are properly archived.
- Business owners or those who work with sensitive information should consider using a more secure backup system that encrypts your files for extra protection.

A graphic designer who works with large files took the time to set up an automatic backup system for all her work. She no longer worries about losing important projects, and this peace of mind has made her more productive.

PRACTICAL EXERCISES: SETTING UP AN ERGONOMIC AND INSPIRING WORKSPACE

With your digital space now decluttered and optimized for efficiency, it's time to shift focus to the physical workspace. This time, the goal is to make it not only functional but also ergonomic and inspiring. Your workspace should be a place you enjoy being where productivity flows naturally and you can tackle your tasks without unnecessary discomfort or distractions.

Whether you work from a dedicated office or a cozy corner in your living room, setting up an ergonomic and aesthetically pleasing workspace can transform your workday.

Let's explore some practical strategies to create a setup that supports both your health and motivation.

Ergonomics 101: Aligning Comfort and Productivity

If you've ever ended the day with a stiff neck, sore back, or aching wrists, chances are your workspace isn't ergonomically designed. Poor ergonomics can take a toll on your body and drain your focus and energy.

Instructions

- **Chair:** Invest in a chair that offers proper lumbar support. You should be sitting up straight, with your feet flat on the floor or a footrest. If you don't have a fancy office chair, use a small cushion to support your lower back.
- **Desk height:** Your desk should allow your arms to rest comfortably at a 90-degree angle. If it is too high, consider an adjustable chair. Too low? Use risers or a stack of books.
- **Monitor placement:** The top of your screen should be positioned at eye level and about an arm's length away. Use a monitor stand or a stack of books to raise it if needed.
- **Keyboard and mouse:** Keep your wrists straight and your hands at or slightly below elbow level. Wrist rests can help prevent strain if you type all day.

Pro tip: If you work on a laptop, consider investing in an external keyboard and mouse to maintain proper alignment.

Lighting Matters: Illuminate Your Workspace Wisely

Lighting isn't just about aesthetics; it affects your energy levels, mood, and even your eye health. Poor lighting can cause eye strain, headaches, and fatigue, making it harder to focus.

Instructions

- **Natural light:** Position your desk near a window if possible, but avoid glare on your screen by angling it perpendicular to the light source.
- **Task lighting:** Add a desk lamp with adjustable brightness to focus light where you need it most. A warm, light tone helps reduce eye strain during late-night work.
- **Ambient lighting:** Keep the overall room well-lit to avoid a stark contrast between your screen and the surrounding space.

Pro tip: If natural light isn't an option, consider full-spectrum light bulbs that mimic daylight to boost your mood and reduce strain.

Personalize Your Space for Inspiration

Your workspace doesn't have to be boring! Incorporate personal touches and design elements that inspire creativity and keep you motivated. The key is to strike a balance between aesthetics and functionality.

Instructions

- **Decorate thoughtfully:** Add a piece of artwork, motivational quotes, or a vision board that aligns with your goals.
- **Plants:** A small indoor plant or succulent can breathe life into your workspace. Studies have shown that having greenery nearby can boost productivity and reduce stress (*How to Stay Active at Home & Improve Your Mental Health During Crisis*, 2022).
- **Color scheme:** Choose colors that energize you. For example, blue is calming, while yellow sparks creativity.
- **Declutter with style:** Use attractive storage solutions, like decorative baskets or trays, to keep essentials within reach without creating visual clutter.

Pro tip: Avoid over-decorating. Too many items can feel chaotic and distract you from your work.

Create a Multi-Zone Workspace

If your home office has enough space, consider setting up distinct zones for different activities. This can help you mentally switch between tasks and avoid monotony.

Instructions

- **Main work zone:** This is where your desk, chair, and computer are set up for focused work.
- **Brainstorming zone:** Add a whiteboard, corkboard, or even just a notebook and pen to jot down ideas and brainstorm freely.
- **Break zone:** If possible, create a small area nearby for quick breaks—a comfy chair with a throw blanket or a yoga mat for stretching.

Pro tip: Even if your space is limited, use visual markers like a rug or different lighting to separate areas for focus versus relaxation.

Manage Cables and Tech Accessories

A tangle of cables and scattered tech accessories looks messy and can be a hassle to navigate. Organizing them is a simple way to make your workspace feel more streamlined and functional.

Instructions

- **Cable management:** Use zip ties, Velcro straps, or cable organizers to bundle and hide cords. You can also attach cables under your desk with adhesive hooks.
- **Docking stations:** Invest in a docking station or hub to keep all your devices connected in one place.
- **Label cords:** Use small labels or tags to identify each cord. This saves you time when something needs to be unplugged or replaced.

Pro tip: Keep a small basket or box for frequently used accessories like chargers, USB drives, and headphones.

Incorporate Movement Into Your Workspace

Sitting for long periods can negatively impact your health and energy levels. Designing your workspace to encourage movement can make a big difference.

Instructions

- **Standing desk:** If possible, invest in a height-adjustable standing desk to switch between sitting and standing throughout the day.
- **Stretching space:** Leave a small, clear area nearby for quick stretches or exercises.
- **Active sitting:** Consider a balance ball chair or a wobble cushion to keep your core engaged while seated.

Pro tip: Set a timer to remind yourself to stand up and move every hour.

With your home office streamlined and organized, it's time to focus on the bathroom, a space that should promote self-care, not stress. Decluttering toiletries and personal items will help create a minimalist, peaceful bathroom routine. We'll also explore maintaining a clean and inviting bathroom space. So, turn to the next page!

7

SIMPLIFYING THE BATHROOM—A SPACE FOR SELF-CARE

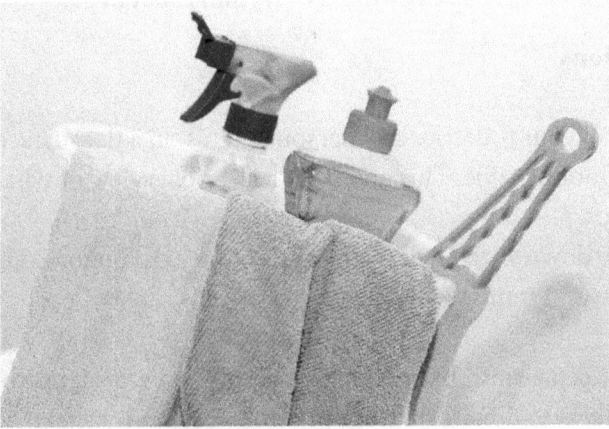

You step into your bathroom early in the morning, hoping for a peaceful start to your day, only to find chaos. The countertop is cluttered with half-empty bottles, stray cotton swabs, and mismatched makeup. You reach for your favorite moisturizer, but it's buried under a pile of products you barely use. Instead of feeling refreshed, you're already frustrated, and the day hasn't even begun.

Sound familiar?

Bathrooms are meant to refresh, recharge, and practice self-care. But when clutter takes over, that calming atmosphere is replaced with stress and frustration. The good news? With a bit of decluttering and smart organization, you can transform the space into a self-care oasis.

Let's begin learning about it in detail.

DECLUTTERING TOILETRIES AND PERSONAL ITEMS

Toiletries and personal items are some of the biggest sources of bathroom clutter, so let's tackle them first.

Start With a Clean Slate

Before organizing, remove everything from your bathroom counters, shelves, and cabinets. Seeing your space empty helps you visualize what you want to keep and where everything should go.

Instructions

- Lay all your toiletries and personal items on a flat surface, like the floor or table. This gives you a clear overview of what you own.
- Wipe down shelves, drawers, and counters to remove dust, spills, and stains.

Pro tip: Keep a trash bag and a box handy—one for items to toss and one for items to donate (like unopened, unused products).

Sort, Purge, and Prioritize

Seeing all your products laid out might surprise you—how did you accumulate so much? It's time to be honest about what you really need and use.

Instructions

- **Sort by category:** Group similar items together—skincare, haircare, oral hygiene, makeup, etc. This helps you see duplicates and prioritize essentials.

- **Check expiration dates:** Skincare and makeup products expire faster than you think. Toss anything that's past its prime—yes, that old mascara and crusty sunscreen need to go!
- **Be realistic:** If you haven't used a product in six months, ask yourself why. Was it an impulse buy that didn't work for you? Is it a product you've outgrown? If you don't love it, let it go.

Pro tip: For those half-used bottles you're reluctant to throw away, commit to using them up before buying replacements.

Limit "Just in Case" Items

We all have those "just in case" products we're holding onto—a travel-sized hairspray, a perfume you don't like but feel guilty throwing away, or a free sample from months ago. Let's be honest—these items just add unnecessary clutter.

Instructions

- **Set a backup limit:** Decide how many backup items are reasonable. For example, one extra toothpaste or shampoo bottle is practical, but five might be excessive.
- **Keep only what you love:** Keep only what you genuinely like and would repurchase. If it doesn't spark joy or serve a clear purpose, it's time to say goodbye.

Pro tip: Create a dedicated spot for travel-sized items. A small box or drawer organizer can keep them tidy and ready for your next trip.

Streamline Your Daily Essentials

Your bathroom should support your daily routines, not overwhelm you with choices. Simplifying your essentials can save time and reduce decision fatigue.

Instructions

- **Identify your essentials:** Determine the products you use daily—think toothbrush, toothpaste, cleanser, moisturizer, deodorant, etc.
- **Give them a home:** Designate a specific spot for these essentials, preferably on the counter or in an easy-to-access drawer.
- **Tuck away extras:** Store less frequently used items (like hair masks or special treatments) out of sight but within reach.

Pro tip: Use small trays or containers to group your daily essentials. This keeps your countertop neat while making everything easily accessible.

Organize by Accessibility and Frequency

Not everything needs to live on your countertop. The key is to organize items based on how often you use them.

Instructions

- **Daily use:** Keep your frequently used items within arm's reach—on the counter, in a drawer, or in a cabinet organizer.
- **Occasional use:** Store less frequently used items, like nail polish or deep conditioners, in higher cabinets or less accessible drawers.
- **Rarely used:** For items like holiday-themed bath products or gift sets, store them in a separate container and revisit them seasonally.

Pro tip: Drawer dividers or small baskets can work wonders for keeping products neatly separated by category.

Rotate and Refresh Regularly

Decluttering is just the beginning—it's important to maintain the order you've created. Plan to revisit your bathroom organization every few months.

Instructions

- **Toss the old:** Check for expired products or items you no longer use.
- **Evaluate your setup:** Reassess your storage solutions—are they still working, or do you need to adjust?
- **Swap seasonal products:** Rotate seasonal items, like summer-specific sunscreens or winter-heavy moisturizers, to keep your routine streamlined.

Pro tip: Use this time to deep-clean your bathroom surfaces and give your space a fresh start.

MAINTAINING A CLEAN AND INVITING BATHROOM

With your toiletries and personal items decluttered, your bathroom is starting to feel lighter and more functional. But as anyone who's been through this process knows, keeping it that way requires consistent effort. A clean and inviting bathroom should feel fresh, welcoming, and ready to serve your self-care routines without adding stress to your life.

Let's explore simple ways to maintain that sense of order and cleanliness, transforming your bathroom into a space you'll genuinely enjoy using every day.

Build Simple Cleaning Habits Into Your Routine

Cleaning your bathroom doesn't have to be an overwhelming chore. Breaking it down into manageable daily, weekly, and monthly tasks is the key to keeping your space spotless.

Instructions

- **Daily:** After brushing your teeth or doing skincare, wipe down your sink and countertop with a microfiber cloth or disinfectant wipe. This prevents buildup and keeps surfaces shining.
- **Weekly:** Clean the mirror, scrub the toilet, and mop the floor. Set a reminder or tie it to an existing routine, like laundry day, to make it a habit.
- **Monthly:** Deep clean the shower or tub, descale faucets, and sanitize overlooked spots like door handles and light switches.

Pro tip: Store a small cleaning caddy under your sink or in a nearby closet with essentials like an all-purpose cleaner, a sponge, and a glass cleaner. Having everything at arm's reach makes it easier to clean on the fly.

One busy professional shared how spending two minutes wiping down surfaces after brushing her teeth each night helped her avoid the dreaded "cleaning day pileup."

Use Storage Solutions to Simplify Cleanup

A clutter-free bathroom is easier to clean. Smart storage solutions make tidying up faster and more efficient.

Instructions

- **Group similar items:** Use baskets or bins to store items together, such as hair products or skincare. Label them for easy identification.
- **Maximize cabinet space:** Invest in stackable containers or tiered shelves to maximize vertical space inside cabinets.
- **Use hooks for towels and robes:** Keeping them off the floor helps them dry more quickly, reducing the chances of mildew.

Pro tip: Clear containers are perfect for under-sink storage, letting you see what you have at a glance.

A stay-at-home parent organized her family's bathroom by assigning each member a color-coded bin for their personal toiletries. This not only kept the space neat but also minimized arguments about missing items.

Keep the Air Fresh and the Atmosphere Relaxing

A clean bathroom isn't just about looks—it should also smell and feel good. Small touches can elevate your bathroom from a utilitarian space to a relaxing retreat.

Instructions

- **Ventilation:** Run the bathroom fan during and after showers to prevent moisture buildup, which can lead to mold and mildew. If possible, open a window for fresh air.
- **Scent:** Use an essential oil diffuser, scented candle, or reed diffuser to keep the air fresh and inviting. Look for calming scents like lavender or eucalyptus.
- **Aesthetics:** Add small decorative touches, like a plant, a pretty soap dish, or a neatly folded stack of towels, to make the space feel cared for.

Pro tip: For natural air purification, consider a bathroom-friendly plant like a snake plant or pothos. They thrive in humid conditions and require little maintenance.

Create a System for Linens and Towels

Towels and linens can quickly clutter a bathroom if not properly managed. Keeping them organized ensures they're clean, accessible, and in good condition.

Instructions

- **Designated storage:** Assign specific storage spots for clean towels—whether it's a shelf, a linen closet, or a decorative basket. Roll towels instead of folding them to save space and give a spa-like vibe.
- **Keep it simple:** Limit the number of towels you keep in the bathroom to avoid overcrowding. A good rule of thumb is two sets per person: one in use and one as a backup.
- **Tackle damp towels:** Immediately remove damp towels from the bathroom to prevent odors or mildew. If you don't have space for a hamper, install a hook or towel bar near the washing machine.

Pro tip: Use matching or coordinating towels for a cohesive and polished look, but prioritize quality over quantity.

For example, one busy professional found that using hooks instead of towel bars gave her more flexibility. It also encouraged family members to hang towels properly after use.

Keep Products Minimal and Rotated

Even after decluttering, it's easy for toiletries to creep back into your bathroom over time. Maintaining a system to manage your products will keep things under control.

Instructions

- **Stick to "one in, one out":** If you buy a new shampoo, finish or discard the old one before opening it.
- **Toss expired products:** Regularly check expiration dates and get rid of anything past its prime immediately.

- **Store extras elsewhere:** Keep bulk buys or less frequently used items, like extra soap or shampoo bottles, in a separate storage area to avoid overcrowding your everyday space.

Pro tip: One stay-at-home parent keeps a small basket of "use-it-up" products on the countertop to remind herself to finish open items before buying new ones.

Address Common Problem Areas Quickly

Little annoyances—like a dripping faucet or a loose shower caddy —can make your bathroom feel less inviting. Tackling these issues as they arise prevents them from becoming bigger problems.

Instructions

- **Fix plumbing issues fast:** Don't ignore issues like slow drains or leaking faucets—address them as soon as possible.
- **Secure loose fixtures:** Tighten wobbly towel bars or cabinet handles before they break.
- **Swap out worn items:** Replace damaged items like shower curtains, bathmats, or toilet seat covers periodically to keep the space looking fresh.

Pro tip: Keep basic tools (like a wrench and screwdriver) in your cleaning caddy for quick fixes.

Set a Maintenance Schedule

The best way to keep your bathroom clean and inviting is to incorporate maintenance into your routine so it becomes second nature.

Instructions

- **Daily:** Dedicate five to ten minutes every day to quick tasks, like wiping down surfaces or emptying the trash.
- **Weekly:** Set aside one longer session each week to tackle deeper cleaning and reorganizing.

- **Every one to two months:** Schedule reminders for less frequent tasks, like replacing the shower liner or checking under the sink for leaks.

Pro tip: If you share the bathroom with others, assign specific tasks to family members to spread the workload.

PRACTICAL EXERCISES: CREATING A MINIMALIST BATHROOM ROUTINE

With your bathroom now clean, organized, and inviting, it's time to take things one step further by simplifying your daily routine.

Let's create a minimalist bathroom routine that fits your lifestyle.

Pare Down Your Daily Essentials

A minimalist bathroom routine starts with identifying the core items you actually use daily. Many of us tend to collect products that sit unused, creating unnecessary clutter and decision fatigue.

Instructions

- **Audit your products:** Lay out everything you use daily for hygiene and skincare. Be honest about what you actually reach for every day.
- **Limit your essentials:** Stick to one product per category (e.g., one shampoo, one cleanser, one moisturizer). Store extras elsewhere to avoid crowding your space.
- **Invest in multi-use products:** Opt for items that serve dual purposes, like a shampoo-conditioner combo or a moisturizer with SPF.

Pro tip: Keep daily-use products in a designated area, such as a shower caddy or a small countertop organizer, to keep them easily accessible.

Design a Morning and Evening Ritual

Minimalism isn't just about reducing products—it's also about simplifying your habits. A well-designed morning and evening routine can make your time in the bathroom feel purposeful and calming.

Instructions

- **Morning:** Focus on the basics—brushing your teeth, washing your face, and applying any skincare or makeup products. Limit your routine to five to ten minutes to start your day efficiently.
- **Evening:** Wind-down by removing makeup, cleansing your face, and brushing your teeth. Consider adding a simple self-care step, like applying a relaxing face mask or using an essential oil roller.

Pro tip: Keep a small basket or tray with everything you need for your morning or evening routine to avoid rummaging through drawers.

Embrace Minimalist Tools and Accessories

Your bathroom tools should support your minimalist goals not clutter your space with multiple gadgets or accessories. Choose versatile, high-quality items.

Instructions

- **Simplify your tools:** Stick to a few essentials, such as a hairbrush, nail clippers, and a reusable razor.
- **Choose sustainable options:** Swap disposable items (like cotton pads or single-use razors) for reusable alternatives, such as washable makeup remover pads or a safety razor.
- **Declutter your shower:** Replace multiple loofahs or sponges with a single high-quality option, like a natural sea sponge.

Pro tip: Before buying a new tool, ask yourself if it will truly simplify your routine or if it's just adding more stuff to manage.

Set Time Limits for Bathroom Activities

Bathroom activities like long showers or extended skincare routines take up more time than you realize. Setting limits ensures your minimalist routine stays practical.

Instructions

- **Speed up skincare:** On busy mornings, stick to a quick cleanse and moisturize routine. Save more indulgent steps, like exfoliation or masks, for the weekend.
- **Stick to a haircare plan:** Set specific days for washing or styling your hair to avoid spending unnecessary time on it daily.

Pro tip: Use the time saved for other morning priorities, like breakfast or preparing for work.

Rotate Non-Daily Self-Care Practices

Not all bathroom activities, like deep conditioning your hair or exfoliating, need to happen daily. By designating specific days for these tasks, you'll keep your routine efficient without sacrificing self-care.

Instructions

- **Choose a weekly schedule:** Assign tasks like hair masks or nail care to a specific day. For example, reserve Sundays for full-body exfoliation and Wednesdays for deep conditioning.
- **Keep it simple:** Avoid adding unnecessary steps just because you feel you "should." Stick to what genuinely benefits you.

Pro tip: Use a sticky note or a digital calendar reminder to stay on track with your self-care schedule.

Minimize Distractions for a Relaxing Atmosphere

To truly embrace a minimalist bathroom routine, it's about creating an environment that encourages focus and relaxation. A clutter-free space enhances your ability to enjoy the moment.

Instructions

- **Eliminate visual clutter:** Keep countertops tidy and store away anything not in use.
- **Add a calming element:** Consider playing soft music or lighting a candle to set a soothing tone during your routine.
- **Turn off notifications:** Leave your phone outside the bathroom to avoid distractions and make the space feel more intentional.

Pro tip: Designate your bathroom as a "no-screen zone" to fully focus on yourself.

Now that you've created a calm space in your bathroom, it's time to tackle the paper piles you've accumulated in your home. The next chapter will guide you through implementing effective filing systems and help you reduce paperwork by leveraging digital solutions. Managing paper clutter doesn't have to be overwhelming, and you'll soon have a system that keeps everything in order.

8

MANAGING PAPER CLUTTER— FROM PILES TO FILES

I magine this: You're in a rush to find an important document. Your child's vaccination record, an overdue bill, or that lease agreement you swore you "put somewhere safe." You check the closest pile of papers, rifling through old receipts and junk mail, only to come up empty-handed. Does it sound familiar?

For most of us, managing paper clutter feels like a never-ending battle. It starts small—a few unopened envelopes, a child's artwork, or old magazines. But before you know it, the piles have taken on a life of their own. Whether they're stashed in a corner, shoved into a junk drawer, or are swallowing your kitchen counter, paper clutter is sneaky. It creates stress along with making your house dirty. Studies show that visual clutter overwhelms the brain, making it harder to focus and increasing anxiety (Sander, 2019).

But, no matter how overwhelming the situation feels, it *is* possible to tame the paper chaos. You just need the right system to transform those piles into a streamlined, functional setup.

Let's start with one simple mindset shift: Every piece of paper in your home has a purpose—or it doesn't. Once you decide where each one belongs (or doesn't belong at all), you'll discover that managing paper isn't as overwhelming as it seems.

IMPLEMENTING EFFECTIVE FILING SYSTEMS

So, how do you go from piles to files? Most filing systems fail because they're too complicated. Have you ever tried setting up a filing system with color-coded folders and labels only to abandon them a week later? You're not alone.

A system only works if it's simple, intuitive, and easy to maintain, especially when you're juggling a busy schedule.

Step 1: Sort Before You Store

Start with a "paper triage." Begin by gathering all your loose papers in one place—yes, all of them. This means pulling out old boxes from your closet, digging through drawers, and tackling that pile on the kitchen counter. Now, go through each piece of paper and sort it into three categories:

1. **Keep:** Essential documents like birth certificates, tax records, and warranties.
2. **Action items:** Bills to pay, forms to fill out, or invitations that need a response.

3. **Toss/shred:** Junk mail, expired coupons, and anything you haven't looked at in six months.

If you're unsure about what to keep, remember this rule of thumb: if it can be replaced (e.g., old bank statements) or you haven't needed it in over a year, it's probably safe to let it go.

Step 2: Create a Filing System That Works for You

Now that you've sorted your papers, it's time to set up your filing system. Here's where many people overcomplicate things. You don't need 20 folders or a fancy filing cabinet to stay organized. Start with just three main categories:

1. **Action folder:** For bills, forms, or anything requiring attention. Keep this in an easily accessible spot, like your desk or kitchen counter.
2. **Reference folder:** For documents you need to keep long-term but don't use often, like tax records, medical files, or insurance policies. These can be stored in a filing cabinet or labeled storage box.
3. **Archive:** For rarely used but essential documents like birth certificates, passports, or legal contracts. Keep these in a secure, waterproof container.

Remember the last time you panicked over a missing document? Imagine your relief if you knew exactly where to find it.

Step 3: Go Digital Wherever Possible

Junk mail alone adds up to over 30 pounds per household every year. On top of that, many companies still send paper bills, bank statements, and receipts by default (Coren, 2023). To cut down on the clutter, switch to digital wherever you can.

Switch to paperless billing, scan important receipts, and use apps like *Evernote* or *Google Drive* to store digital copies of documents. Not tech-savvy? It's as simple as taking a photo with your phone and saving it in a dedicated folder.

Name your digital files in a way that makes them easy to find later. For example, instead of "IMG_1234," label a scanned receipt as "Grocery Receipt_01-15-2025."

Step 4: Establish a Maintenance Routine

Here's the thing about paper: it doesn't stop coming—new mail, school papers, and receipts. Without a system, it can take over fast. Set aside just five minutes a day (or 15 minutes once a week) to go through incoming papers.

When the mail comes in, immediately sort it into three piles: keep (file), act (add to your to-do list), or toss (recycle or shred). By staying on top of it, you'll prevent those overwhelming piles from building up again.

Step 5: Use Tools That Simplify Your Life

Make your system easier to navigate by using clear folders or color-coded labels. For quick access to daily paperwork, try a wall-mounted organizer or a desktop tray with separate sections for "To Do," "To Pay," and "To File."

And don't underestimate the power of a good shredder! Shredding old documents not only reduces clutter but also protects you from identity theft.

Dani, a stay-at-home mom of three, used to keep all her kids' school papers, medical forms, and bills in one big pile on the kitchen counter. It wasn't until she missed a payment on her electric bill—lost in the shuffle—that she decided to make a change.

She set up a simple filing system: one folder for kids' paperwork, another for household bills, and a third for medical records. Then, she scanned old documents and kept digital copies in a cloud storage app. Now, instead of spending hours searching for what she needs, she finds it in seconds.

REDUCING PAPERWORK THROUGH DIGITAL SOLUTIONS

What's one of the most effective ways to reduce paper clutter? Go digital. We've already touched briefly on scanning and storing documents digitally in the previous section, but let's find out how going digital can completely transform how you manage paperwork.

The idea of "going paperless" might sound daunting, especially if you've spent years relying on physical documents. But once you get the hang of it, you'll wonder why you didn't make the switch sooner. Plus, with so many apps, tools, and cloud storage solutions available today, reducing your paperwork has never been easier.

Step 1: Take Advantage of Paperless Billing

One of the simplest ways to reduce the influx of paper into your home is by signing up for paperless billing. Most service providers, banks, utilities, and even subscription services offer the option to receive bills and statements via email instead of snail mail.

Going paperless cuts down on clutter and helps you stay organized. Instead of rummaging through a pile of envelopes, you'll have all your bills stored neatly in your inbox. To stay on top of things, create a dedicated email folder or label (e.g., "Bills") and file incoming statements there immediately.

Pro tip: Set up automatic payments to avoid late fees. Set calendar reminders for due dates so you're always in control of your finances.

Step 2: Use Cloud Storage for Important Documents

Cloud storage makes it easy to access your documents anytime, anywhere—whether you're at home, at work, or even on vacation. Platforms like *Google Drive, Dropbox,* and *OneDrive* allow you to store digital copies of important files securely.

Start by scanning essential documents like tax returns, insurance policies, or your kids' report cards. No scanner? Your smartphone works just fine. Apps like *Adobe Scan* or *CamScanner* let you create high-quality PDFs in seconds. Once uploaded, organize your files into clearly labeled folders (e.g., "Medical Records," "Work Documents") so they're easy to find later.

Pro tip: Make sure you use strong passwords and enable two-factor authentication for your cloud accounts to keep sensitive information secure.

Step 3: Digitize Receipts and Warranties

Receipts and warranties pile up fast and often go missing when you need them most. Instead of holding on to stacks of faded paper receipts, consider digitizing them.

Use apps like *Expensify* or *Shoeboxed* to snap photos of receipts and automatically organize them by date, category, or vendor—perfect for tracking expenses for work or taxes. For warranties, set up a digital folder labeled "Warranties" and upload scanned copies along with the product's purchase date and serial number.

Imagine your blender breaks down a year after purchase. Instead of scrambling to find the warranty in a drawer full of random papers, you can quickly pull it up on your phone and resolve the issue in minutes.

Step 4: Automate Forms and Signatures

Still printing out forms, signing them, and scanning them?

Save yourself the hassle by using e-signature tools like *DocuSign, HelloSign,* or *Adobe Acrobat,* which let you fill out, sign, and send documents electronically—all without touching a single piece of paper.

This is ideal for busy professionals who deal with contracts, permission slips, or any kind of paperwork that needs a quick turnaround. Plus, most e-signature platforms are legally recognized, so you don't have to worry about whether they'll hold up in official situations.

Step 5: Manage Your Digital Inbox

While going digital reduces physical clutter, it's important to keep your digital spaces organized, too. A messy inbox is just as stressful as a pile of papers on your desk.

Start by unsubscribing from newsletters, promotional emails, or services you no longer use. You can do this manually or use tools like *Unroll.Me*. Then, create folders or labels for different categories (e.g., "Work," "Personal," "Receipts") and file emails as they come in.

If you're overwhelmed by unread emails, set aside time to tackle them in batches. Aim for "inbox zero"—or at least a manageable inbox that doesn't feel like it's spiraling out of control.

Will, a freelance graphic designer, was drowning in invoices, contracts, and client notes. By switching to digital solutions, he cut his paper clutter by 80%. Now, he stores all his client files in *Google Drive*, tracks project deadlines in *Trello,* and sends invoices using a digital accounting tool. Not only is his workspace cleaner, but his workflow is more efficient, too.

Practical Exercises: Setting Up a Paper Management System

Exercise 1

Step 1: Sort Your Paper Piles

Before you can set up an effective paper management system, you need to tackle the piles. This might seem overwhelming at first, but breaking it down into smaller tasks makes it manageable.

Gather all the paper you currently have lying around—whether it's on your desk, on your kitchen counter, or in a drawer. Then, go through each pile and categorize the papers using broad categories like:

- **Important** (tax documents, contracts, medical bills)
- **To-do** (items that require action or attention)
- **Reference** (manuals, guides, receipts)
- **Shred** (old, irrelevant documents)

This a moment to consider what types of papers tend to pile up for you. Are work documents overwhelming? Or perhaps medical and personal finance documents are where things get messy? Recognizing patterns will help you set up the best system.

Step 2: Designate Paper Categories and Storage

Once you've sorted your papers, it's time to create a simple filing system. Grab a few basic supplies: file folders, a filing cabinet (or portable file box), and labels. Use color-coded folders or a label maker to help you quickly find what you need later.

Start by creating primary categories based on your previous sorting. You might use folders like:

- bills and financials
- health and insurance
- work projects
- home maintenance

Break folders into subcategories if needed. For example, under "Bills and Financials," create separate folders for utilities, credit cards, and taxes. Make sure everything has a designated place so that once you start filing documents, you'll always know where to put them.

Step 3: Establish a "Paper Flow" Routine

With your system in place, the key is to maintain it. To prevent clutter,, set aside 10-15 minutes at the end of each day or week to go through new paperwork. As things come in, immediately sort them into your filing system or scan them for digital storage.

This daily ritual prevents paper from piling up and ensures that you stay on top of everything. Plus, it reduces mental clutter—you won't find yourself scrambling to find a bill or document at the last minute.

Step 4: Keep Your System Flexible and Easy to Adjust

Your paper needs will change as life does. Be open to adjusting your system over time. Maybe you find that one category can be expanded or that you're receiving less physical mail now that you've gone paperless.

Check in with your paper system every few months and ask yourself:

- Are there any categories you can eliminate?
- Is there a section that needs more structure?
- Are you able to easily find what you need when you need it?

Small tweaks will keep your paper management system running smoothly and will allow you to adapt it as your life and priorities shift.

Exercise 2: The Paperless Week Challenge

Challenge yourself! Take a week to reduce the amount of paper coming into your life by going paperless where possible. This encourages finding digital alternatives to cut down on paperwork.

Steps

1. **Identify paper alternatives:** Track all the papers you receive in a week (e.g., bills, notices, magazine subscriptions, school/work documents). For each type of paper, research and implement a digital alternative (e.g., signing up for e-billing, using digital magazines, storing receipts in apps, etc.).
2. **Set boundaries:** Let your family or coworkers know that

you're going paperless for the week, and encourage them to help reduce unnecessary paper.

3. **Track your success:** Keep a record of how much paper you've replaced (e.g., how many bills, magazines, or documents were handled digitally instead).

4. **Reflect and continue:** After the week, review how the challenge went. Which digital solutions worked best for you? Keep using them, and consider extending the challenge for another week or month.

This exercise helps you get rid of paper clutter for good by shifting to digital solutions, making it easier to manage your documents in the future.

Exercise 3: The Shred It or File It Session

This exercise helps you clear out unnecessary papers while ensuring important documents are safely filed.

Steps

1. **Set a timer:** Grab your pile of papers and set a timer for 30 minutes (or longer if needed). The key here is to work in timed sprints so you don't feel overwhelmed.

2. **Sort your papers:** As you go through the stack, quickly decide: does this paper need to be shredded (expired bills, old bank statements, etc.) or filed (legal documents, insurance papers, medical records)?
   - **Shred:** Immediately shred papers that are no longer needed or have sensitive information.
   - **File:** File important documents according to your pre-established filing system.

3. **Organize as you go:** As you sort, label your folders clearly (e.g., "Tax Documents," "Medical Bills," "Receipts," etc.). Make sure everything has a designated place.

4. **Take action:** Once the session is over, make sure your filing

system—whether physical or digital—is organized and ready for the next session.

By making quick decisions about each paper, you can move toward a clutter-free, organized system while clearing out unnecessary documents.

With your paper clutter under control, let's move on to maintaining the organized state of your home through sustainable habits in the next chapter.

9

MAINTAINING YOUR ORGANIZED HOME—SUSTAINABLE HABITS

W hy is it so easy to get your home organized but difficult to keep it that way? Between a busy work schedule, kids' activities, and constant emails and phone calls, life tends to pile up and disrupt even the best-laid plans. But the truth is, maintaining an organized home is not about a one-time overhaul—it's about creating routines that keep the clutter at bay.

So, how do you make sure that your home stays organized, even when life gets hectic? The answer lies in routines. By establishing daily and weekly rituals, you can easily integrate organization into your life, ensuring your home remains a sanctuary rather than a source of stress.

Let's learn to set and maintain routines!

ESTABLISHING DAILY AND WEEKLY ROUTINES

Many people see organizing as a monumental task, a big spring cleaning, or an all-day Saturday spent decluttering. But it doesn't have to be this way. A few small, manageable steps each day can keep your home looking tidy and well-kept without feeling overwhelmed.

A quick 10-minute tidy-up in the morning can set the tone for a more productive, clutter-free environment. Cleaning doesn't have to take hours; just tackling a few key areas each day can make a huge difference. Try putting away dishes after breakfast, wiping down counters, or straightening up the living room before you head out the door. These small habits help keep clutter from accumulating in the first place, saving you time and energy later in the week.

One thing to remember is that routines don't have to be rigid. They should fit into your natural rhythm. If mornings are too chaotic, shift your focus to the evenings, where you can unwind by tidying up.

Another way to maintain order is through weekly rituals. Set aside time each week on Sunday mornings or Friday afternoons to do a quick sweep of areas that tend to gather clutter. Use this time to go through mail, organize your pantry, or give your bathroom counters a good wipe-down. These small acts will keep your home looking fresh without taking up too much of your time.

Remember, consistency is key. If you miss a day or two, don't beat yourself up. The goal isn't perfection. It's progress. Build a routine that works for you and your lifestyle.

If you are very busy, set clear boundaries with the family about certain areas of the house. For example, designate a "home office zone" that's off-limits for playtime or personal projects. This keeps your workspace from turning into a cluttered mess of papers and toys by the end of the week.

The beauty of daily and weekly routines is that they don't require hours of organizing. They're about spending just a few minutes every day to keep things in order. It's not about perfection—it's about control. When you tackle small tasks consistently, you can maintain an organized home without feeling like it's a never-ending battle.

Imagine never needing major cleaning marathons by simply keeping up with small tasks each day. Wouldn't that feel like a win? Daily and weekly rituals keep your home organized without adding stress to your already busy life.

Having established daily and weekly routines to keep your home organized, there's one crucial element that can make or break your efforts: involving your family members. Between work, home responsibilities, and possibly caring for kids or pets, managing the organization on your own can be overwhelming. But when everyone in the household pitches in, maintaining an organized home becomes not just doable but sustainable.

It's tempting to think, "I'll just do it myself—it's faster," but in the long run, this approach only leads to burnout. Plus, it prevents others from learning essential skills for organization and maintenance. So, how do you get everyone on board?

INVOLVING FAMILY MEMBERS IN THE PROCESS

It all starts with communication. Organizing your home isn't a solo job—it's a team effort. Whether you're managing a busy household with kids or a shared living space with a partner, everyone can contribute in their own way. Start by ensuring expectations are clear. It's not about giving orders; it's about building a shared vision for how the home can function smoothly together.

For example, on a deep cleaning day, get the kids involved by assigning them age-appropriate chores. Your seven-year-old can help with vacuuming or putting away their toys, while your ten-year-old might be in charge of wiping down surfaces or organizing bookshelves.

The goal is to keep things manageable and fun. When kids feel included, they're more likely to buy into the idea of maintaining a tidy space. Plus, this teaches lifelong habits. When tasks are broken down into smaller, bite-sized pieces, they feel much less daunting.

Involving family members doesn't just apply to children, though. If you have a partner, shared responsibilities are key for maintaining the organization. Rather than one person handling the dishes, laundry, or taking out the trash, consider splitting these chores so that both of you contribute equally. When everyone shares the load, it fosters teamwork and prevents one person from feeling over-whelmed.

But let's face it: sometimes, family members don't naturally pitch in. If that happens, discuss why organization is important to you and how everyone can help. Make it about the entire household, not just one person. Perhaps organizing will make mornings run smoother, or it'll reduce stress and help everyone feel more at peace in their space.

Even if you're living alone or with a roommate, you can still involve others in the process. Setting clear expectations for shared spaces, like a kitchen or living room, is key to keeping things running smoothly. Set up a simple plan where each person has a responsibility for keeping their own area tidy and contributing to the overall cleanliness of the shared spaces.

Once roles are established, it's important to follow through. Keep daily and weekly responsibilities clear and check in with each other regularly. This doesn't mean micromanaging but rather supporting one another and celebrating small wins.

A weekly household meeting works particularly well. Keep it short and simple—just a quick check-in to see what's working, what isn't, and how everyone can adjust. Use these meetings to discuss the upcoming week's schedule, which can help to allocate chores around busy events or obligations. This way, everyone knows what's expected and when.

For example, if your partner has an upcoming business trip, they might handle extra chores before they go, or you can plan to handle the organization of shared spaces during the week. Being transparent about schedules ensures that responsibilities aren't forgotten and keeps the process moving.

Creating a Shared Organizational System

To make this all work, create a shared system that everyone can follow. This means specific places for items, designated activity zones, and clear expectations for daily upkeep. The goal is to make it so simple that everyone can participate with ease.

For instance, set up a "drop zone" by the door where everyone can place their keys, bags, or shoes so clutter stays contained. Everyone knows where their items go, and it prevents those little piles from growing into bigger problems.

A shared calendar—whether digital or physical—helps everyone see what's happening in the week ahead. This allows them to plan their time accordingly and contribute to the home's organization without confusion. It's like having a roadmap that everyone follows.

Make It a Positive Experience

When involving your family in the organization process, find ways to make it fun. Turn organizing into a game with your kids; see who can pick up the most toys in five minutes or who can dust the fastest. You can even reward yourselves with something small, like a movie night or a treat, for staying on top of your routines.

For adults, organizing doesn't have to feel like a never-ending task. Play music while you tidy up or schedule a "power hour" where everyone tackles a specific task for 60 minutes. You'll be amazed at how much you can accomplish when you make it a team effort and bring some energy into the mix.

Remember, the goal isn't perfection but rather a well-maintained one that everyone feels responsible for. When family members are actively involved, they're more likely to stick to the routines you've set up. And when your home is organized, it feels like a place of calm and order, not chaos.

PRACTICAL EXERCISE: CREATING A PERSONALIZED MAINTENANCE CHECKLIST

With your family members on board and established routines that work for everyone, it's time to make sure that these habits stay in motion. One powerful way to keep your home organized and ensure consistency is by creating a *personalized maintenance checklist*. Think of it as your roadmap, helping you track daily, weekly, and monthly tasks so everyone knows exactly what needs to be done—and when.

The goal of a maintenance checklist is simple: to keep you and your family on track without feeling overwhelmed by the tasks at hand. Whether you're managing a busy career, a household full of kids, or a combination of both, a checklist is a practical, visual tool that keeps organization at the forefront of your mind.

Step 1: Identify the Key Areas in Your Home

Begin by identifying key areas in your home that need regular attention. You can do this by walking through each room and listing the main tasks that help maintain cleanliness and organization.

For example:

- **Kitchen:** Wipe down counters, load/unload the dishwasher, clear the dining table, wipe the stove after cooking, empty the trash.
- **Living room:** Vacuum the floor, fluff pillows, straighten furniture, wipe down coffee tables, organize remote controls and magazines.
- **Bathrooms:** Wipe mirrors, disinfect counters, empty the trash, change out towels, and clean the sink and toilet.
- **Bedrooms:** Make the bed, pick up clothes, vacuum the floor, dust furniture, and organize nightstands.

When creating your checklist, it's important to include *everything*— even the smaller tasks that might get overlooked, like wiping down light switches or organizing junk drawers. Covering all the areas that need upkeep, you can ensure that nothing slips through the cracks.

Step 2: Break Tasks Down into Daily, Weekly, and Monthly Categories

Next, sort tasks by frequency: daily, weekly, and monthly. This helps you prioritize what needs to be tackled every day versus what can wait a bit longer.

- **Daily tasks:** These are tasks that help maintain a general sense of tidiness and prevent clutter from building up.
  - Example: "Make the bed every morning," "Wash dishes after every meal," "Wipe down bathroom counters after use."
- **Weekly tasks:** These tasks require more time and effort and should be done once a week to ensure that areas don't get neglected.
  - Example: "Vacuum living room," "Clean the bathroom sinks and mirrors," "Dust surfaces in the bedrooms."
- **Monthly tasks:** These tasks are more intensive, often requiring a bit more time and effort, but they help maintain your home's deep cleaning and organization.
  - Example: "Wash windows," "Organize the pantry," "Wipe down baseboards," "Deep clean the fridge."

You don't need to overthink this step—just make sure that your checklist reflects the real needs of your home. Start by considering what you *already* do and how you can group those tasks effectively.

Step 3: Customize the Checklist to Fit Your Family's Schedule

Now it's time to customize your checklist to your family's specific routines. A personalized checklist is most effective when it works within your lifestyle, not the other way around.

For example, if mornings are hectic, tasks like wiping down counters or making the bed might need to happen in the evening instead. Give kids certain daily chores, like picking up their toys or putting away dishes. If your partner works from home, they can tackle the office space while you handle the kitchen.

Use a digital tool or app to easily manage the checklist. Many apps allow you to set reminders and share tasks so everyone in the household knows what needs to be done. A whiteboard in a common area, where you write down the daily and weekly tasks, allows everyone to check them off as they go.

Example of a Personalized Maintenance Checklist

- **Monday:**
    - **Daily:** make bed, do dishes, wipe down kitchen counters
    - **Weekly:** vacuum living room, dust furniture
    - **Monthly:** clean windows in the living room
- **Tuesday:**
    - **Daily:** make bed, do dishes, tidy up bedrooms
    - **Weekly:** clean bathroom sinks, change towels in bathrooms
    - **Monthly:** organize pantry
- **Wednesday:**
    - **Daily:** make bed, do dishes, wipe down bathroom counters
    - **Weekly:** vacuum bedrooms, clean mirrors
    - **Monthly:** wipe down baseboards

This checklist gives you a clear view of what needs to be done daily, weekly, or monthly. Keep it realistic; there's no need to overstuff the list, especially if you're already doing things on a regular basis.

Step 4: Set Up a System for Tracking Progress

With your checklist ready, it's time to implement a system for tracking progress. One of the easiest ways to do this is through a reward-based system or simply by checking off tasks as they get completed.

Consistency is key—encourage everyone in the house to make a habit of checking off the list. Whether a checklist on the fridge or a shared digital document, the key is to make sure everyone sees their progress and stays motivated.

Tie weekly task completion to a small reward—something everyone looks forward to—like a family movie night, an outing, or a small treat. It's about creating positive reinforcement and making maintaining your home feel less like a chore and more like a shared achievement.

Step 5: Adjust as Needed and Keep It Flexible

Life is unpredictable, and sometimes, your checklist should adapt to it. That's perfectly normal! The key is to stay flexible with your approach. If one week is busier than usual, it's okay to push some tasks to the next week. However, if you notice certain tasks aren't being done consistently, it may be a sign that they need to be adjusted or reassigned.

For example, the living room is always cluttered, but the kids' rooms stay tidy; have them take on more responsibility for keeping the living room organized. Refining the checklist is an ongoing process to make sure that it continues to work for your unique lifestyle.

With a personalized maintenance checklist, you'll be able to stay on top of your home's organization without constantly feeling like you're cleaning up someone else's mess. And when everyone knows what's expected and has a clear role, your home will run more smoothly, helping everyone feel more at ease in their space.

Having an organized drop zone helps control clutter and ensures that essential items are always easy to find.

You've made it to the finish line! Now, it's time to celebrate your transformation and take a moment to reflect on your journey. You've decluttered, organized, and streamlined your home, and now you get to enjoy the fruits of your labor. In the next, you'll learn how to celebrate your progress.

10

CELEBRATING YOUR SUCCESS— ENJOYING YOUR CLUTTER- FREE LIFE

Take a moment to recognize how much your life has shifted since you started organizing your home. At first, the changes may have seemed small, but now that you're living in a more clutter-free space, you realize that your home feels lighter, more functional, and even more enjoyable to be in. The beauty of this transformation lies in the sense of calm and accomplishment—you've worked hard to create an environment that supports your life, your goals, and your well-being.

Now that clutter no longer takes up precious space, both physically and mentally, pause and *reflect on your transition*. This chapter is all about celebrating how far you've come and recognizing the progress you've made along the way.

Looking back, appreciate the effort it took to get here, acknowledge the challenges you overcame, and take pride in the new, more organized version of your life. It's not just about the results—though those are certainly worth celebrating—this journey is about the growth you've experienced as you've committed to creating sustainable habits.

RECOGNIZING HOW FAR YOU'VE COME

Remember when you first started? Were you overwhelmed by the mess? Did it feel like an impossible task to declutter and maintain order? It's easy to forget how much has changed as you slip into your new routines and begin to reap the benefits of an organized home. But taking a moment to reflect on how much you've achieved can give you a huge sense of satisfaction and motivation to continue.

You used to spend hours each week searching for things in a disorganized home, now you might find that you can easily locate what you need, saving time and reducing stress. Maybe your family members are more involved, and chores are being shared more evenly, or perhaps you've created systems that allow your space to stay neat with minimal effort. These are all victories worth celebrating.

Want to truly see your progress? Create a "before and after" snapshot. Take a moment to revisit pictures or notes from when you started. Look at the cluttered spaces that used to overwhelm you, and then compare them to how they look now. The changes might not always be immediately obvious day-to-day, but when you take a step back, you'll see just how far you've come.

Acknowledge the Challenges You've Overcome

Organizing your home isn't always easy—it takes time, effort, and persistence. Along the way, there were probably moments when you felt frustrated or doubted whether it was worth it. Maybe you had setbacks, or life got in the way, but the important part is that you kept going.

Reflect on those challenges. Maybe the task seemed overwhelming at times, and you had to work through a few obstacles. Perhaps certain habits were harder to change than others. Each challenge you faced was an opportunity for growth. You overcame them, and you became more resilient and determined to stay the course. Whether it was organizing the kitchen or setting up routines for your family, each step you took was part of the bigger transformation.

Remember how great it felt to tackle it head-on and make a real difference. Those small victories add up, and they remind you that you are capable of more than you think.

Celebrate Your Success, Big and Small

It's easy to rush through life without acknowledging your wins, especially when there's always more to do. But your journey toward a more organized life deserves to be celebrated. Whether you've mastered the art of keeping your home tidy or have finally overcome the overwhelming feeling of clutter, give yourself credit for your hard work.

Consider celebrating in small ways—treat yourself to something you've been wanting, take a day to relax and enjoy your space, or share your achievements with others who've supported you along the way. These celebrations reinforce the positive changes and progress you've made. No matter how small, it is worth acknowledging.

The truth is, a clutter-free home isn't just about aesthetics. It's also about creating an environment that helps you thrive. It's the peace of mind that comes with knowing you're in control of your space and your life. Reflecting on your transformation, you not only acknowledge your success, but you also strengthen your commitment to maintaining it long-term.

Now, as you enjoy your clutter-free life, take a moment to appreciate all the hard work it took to get here. You've come a long way, and that's something worth celebrating!

SETTING NEW GOALS FOR CONTINUOUS IMPROVEMENT

As you look around your transformed space, you might find yourself wondering: *What's next?* Achieving a clutter-free home and creating new, sustainable habits is a huge accomplishment, but maintaining and building on those results is key to long-term success. The good news? A little intentional goal-setting can continue to improve your space, habits, and routines—keeping your home organized and your life in balance.

Now that you've settled into a rhythm and established a solid foundation, it's time to think about the next steps. This section will guide you through the process of setting new goals that promote continuous improvement. Your home is in a good place, but that's just the beginning.

Let's learn how you can take your current momentum and transform it into ongoing growth.

Look Back to Look Forward

Before setting new goals, pause to reflect on what's been working well and acknowledge areas that still need attention. This self-reflection is key to understanding where you stand and what needs further development.

For example, maybe your living room is clutter-free, but you still struggle with staying on top of laundry. Recognizing where you've been successful and where there's room for growth will allow you to set goals that are more targeted and achievable.

A simple journal or checklist where you can note what's working and what isn't can make this process easier and give you a clear starting point for creating your new goals.

Be Specific With Your Goals

Once you've reflected on your progress, it's time to set new goals. The best goals are specific and actionable. Instead of saying, "I want to keep my home organized," try, "I will clear all surfaces in my living room every night before bed."

Specificity allows you to create an actionable plan and gives you a clear target to work toward. You can apply this principle to different areas of your life, from decluttering a particular room to establishing routines for regular home maintenance.

Set Realistic and Achievable Goals

It's tempting to set ambitious goals, but it's also important to keep them realistic. Setting the bar too high can feel overwhelming and cause you to lose motivation. Instead, focus on what you can realistically achieve in the next few months.

For example, if you've been struggling with keeping your workspace organized, create a realistic goal: "I will clean and organize my desk every Friday afternoon." Consistently meeting smaller goals will give you the confidence to tackle more challenging tasks later.

Realistic goals are easier to maintain over time. Achieving them consistently reinforces the habits you're trying to build and gives you a sense of accomplishment.

Incorporate the Process Into Your Routine

Don't think of goal-setting as a one-time task; treat it as a part of your ongoing routine. This mindset will keep you focused on continuous improvement rather than thinking you've reached a point of perfection.

Incorporate goal-setting into your routine by dedicating a few minutes each week to reviewing your goals and progress. This keeps you accountable and gives you the chance to adjust your goals as necessary. You might discover that you can make more progress in a certain area or that a specific goal needs tweaking.

Create Micro-Goals for Big Tasks

Larger tasks can feel daunting and make it easy for you to procrastinate. Break down those big tasks into smaller, more manageable steps, what we call "micro-goals." By focusing on one small action at a time, you can make substantial progress without feeling overwhelmed.

For example, if your larger goal is to organize your entire closet, break it down like this:

- **Week 1:** Sort through shoes and donate or discard what you no longer wear.
- **Week 2:** Organize all shirts and fold them neatly, donating any you no longer need.
- **Week 3:** Work through pants and skirts, focusing on getting rid of anything that doesn't fit or that you haven't worn in a year.

By breaking the process down, you'll feel less overwhelmed and more motivated to keep going. Plus, each small win will keep your momentum going, helping you feel like you're always moving forward.

Make Adjustments Along the Way

While it's important to set goals, it's equally important to stay flexible and make adjustments when needed. Life happens, unexpected things come up, priorities shift, and sometimes, you just need to reassess your goals.

Say your goal is to organize your pantry, but your kitchen is too small to keep everything neat in one place. Instead, adjust your goal to better suit your space or needs. The goal should work for you, not the other way around.

If a full pantry overhaul will require more time and energy than you initially thought, break it into smaller tasks or adjust your timeline. Flexibility keeps you from feeling like a failure if things don't go exactly as planned.

Celebrate Milestones and Progress

As you work toward your new goals, take time to celebrate your progress, no matter how small. Each step forward is an achievement, and acknowledging that can keep you motivated. It's easy to forget to celebrate in the rush of everyday life, but taking the time to recognize your wins gives you the momentum to continue.

Refine and Adjust Your Goals Regularly

Remember, goal-setting is an ongoing process. What works for you now might need refining down the road. Continue to check in every few months to assess whether your goals are still relevant or if they need to be adjusted to better reflect your current situation.

Regular check-ins allow you to stay on top of your goals and ensure that they align with your current life. Reaching a goal doesn't mean you stop setting new ones. Continuous improvement is all about staying engaged and adapting as you evolve.

By continually setting new goals, you are not only maintaining your progress but also creating a lifestyle of organization and growth. Your home will stay organized, your routines will stay efficient, and you'll continue to feel empowered by the process.

PRACTICAL EXERCISE: DESIGNING A GRATITUDE RITUAL FOR YOUR HOME

As you strive for continuous improvement in your home and daily routines, it's equally important to pause and reflect on the present. Celebrating small wins and staying motivated are crucial for keeping the momentum going. One way to deepen your connection with your organized space is through gratitude. Focus on what you're grateful for in your home and your life; it fosters a sense of joy and appreciation and can encourage you to maintain your home's organization and keep a positive mindset.

Incorporating gratitude rituals into your daily routine can help you stay connected to your space and remind yourself why it's worth the effort. Whether starting small or aiming for a big shift, these rituals can help anchor your journey. Let's explore five practical exercises to design a gratitude ritual for your home, helping you stay grounded and connected to your progress.

Gratitude Journal for Your Home

A simple and effective way to cultivate gratitude is by journaling. Take five minutes every day to write down three things you're grateful for in your home. It could be the comfort of your bed or the peaceful vibe in your living room after you've tidied up. The key is to really focus on what feels good about your environment and the efforts you've put into creating it.

Instructions

1. Set a time each day (morning or evening) to jot down your gratitude list.
2. Reflect on small moments of peace, joy, or pride in your home.
3. Use your journal as a tool to track your emotional connection to your space over time.
4. Share any thoughts or reflections on your progress, noting how it enhances your daily routine.

As you develop this practice, you'll begin to notice more details around you to be thankful for, and it will reinforce the positive aspects of your organized space.

Gratitude Walk Around Your Home

A gratitude walk is a simple mindfulness exercise—walk through your home and mentally acknowledge the positive aspects of each space. Whether your favorite chair, the scent of fresh flowers in the kitchen, or the peaceful ambience of your bedroom, allow yourself to experience a sense of appreciation as you walk.

Instructions

1. Begin at the entrance of your home and take a slow, deliberate walk through each room.
2. As you walk, pause at each space and mentally express gratitude for the specific qualities or items in that room that bring you joy or comfort.
3. Pay attention to how your energy shifts as you focus on gratitude rather than the tasks or messes you may be trying to avoid.
4. End your walk with a moment of reflection on the overall feeling in your home, appreciating all the progress you've made.

This ritual can help you refocus on the positives in your environment, reinforcing the sense of peace and purpose that comes with an organized space.

Morning Gratitude Affirmations

Starting your day with positive affirmations helps cultivate a mindset of gratitude and appreciation for your living space.

Instructions

1. As soon as you wake up, take a deep breath and focus on the comfort of your home.
2. Say or write down three affirmations about your home, such as:
   a. "I am grateful for the safety and warmth of my home."
   b. "My space supports and nurtures me."
   c. "Every day, my home becomes more peaceful and organized."
3. Repeat these affirmations daily to set a positive tone for your day.

By making this a habit, you'll reinforce feelings of gratitude and cultivate a more intentional relationship with your space.

Acts of Gratitude for Your Home

Expressing gratitude through action can deepen your appreciation for your space and inspire you to care for it with love.

Instructions

1. Choose a simple act of care for your home each day, such as:
   a. Wiping down surfaces with intention and appreciation.
   b. Fluffing pillows and tidying up with a grateful mindset.
   c. Lighting a candle or playing calming music to create a positive atmosphere.
2. As you perform these small acts, take a moment to acknowledge how they contribute to your well-being.

This mindful approach helps turn everyday maintenance into a meaningful gratitude practice.

A Gratitude Corner for Guests

Sharing gratitude with loved ones can amplify its effect and create a welcoming, appreciative environment.

Instructions

- Designate a small area in your home where guests can leave notes of gratitude.
- Provide a small notebook, sticky notes, or a jar with paper and pens.
- Encourage visitors to write something they're grateful for—whether about the home, the people in it, or their experience during their visit.
- Periodically read these notes to reflect on the joy and appreciation shared in your space.

This exercise promotes a culture of gratitude in your home and strengthens connections with those who enter it.

Decluttering With Gratitude

Decluttering often feels like a tedious task, but with a gratitude mindset, it can become an act of appreciation rather than a chore. The idea is to thank each item you choose to keep or part with, acknowledging how it served you or helped create your ideal space.

Instructions

1. As you declutter a particular area (such as your closet or kitchen counter), take a moment to pause and reflect on each item.
2. If it's something you want to keep, thank it for its usefulness or beauty. If it's something you're letting go of, thank it for its role in your life and recognize that it's time for a change.
3. Continue this process throughout your home as you move through each item or category, whether it's clothing, books, or kitchenware.

4. Allow yourself to feel grateful for the space that is being created and the organization that comes with it.

By infusing gratitude into decluttering, you shift the focus from the effort required to let go of things to a celebration of what you've already achieved and the new possibilities your space will offer.

Creating a Gratitude-Altar or Space

A gratitude altar is a special space where you display items that symbolize what you're thankful for in your life and home. It might be a small table, a shelf, or a corner of a room—anywhere you feel inspired to honor your progress and the positive energy in your home.

Instructions

1. Find a small area in your home that feels inviting and peaceful.
2. Gather meaningful items, such as photographs, candles, plants, or objects that hold sentimental value, and place them on the altar.
3. Each time you pass by or interact with this space, take a moment to reflect on what each item represents and why you're grateful for it.
4. Regularly update or rotate the items on your altar to reflect new achievements or things you're currently appreciating in your life.

This exercise will give you a designated space to focus on gratitude while also enhancing the visual appeal of your home. It can serve as a reminder of how far you've come and what you've created.

Gratitude Ritual Before Bed

Wind down with a short gratitude ritual before to end your day on a positive note. Reflecting on your home and your day in a peaceful moment can help you relax, appreciate your space, and set the tone for a restful night.

Instructions

1. Just before bed, sit quietly in your favorite space in your home (it could be the living room, your bedroom, or anywhere you feel comfortable).
2. Close your eyes and take a few deep breaths, grounding yourself in the moment.
3. Think about the things you're grateful for in your home— whether it's the cozy bed, the fresh air, or simply the calm of the evening.
4. As you breathe deeply, focus on the positive energy that your organized home brings into your life.

This simple ritual will help you wind down while strengthening your connection with your home, making it a sanctuary of peace and contentment.

Take a moment to celebrate the calm, the order, and the peace you've worked so hard to create. As you continue your journey, let the clarity you've found in your space be a reflection of the clarity you carry within. Enjoy your clutter-free life. It's a reflection of the balance and well-being you've worked so hard to cultivate. As you embrace your new habits and goals, remember that every step forward is a step toward a more organized, fulfilling life. You've earned this success— now, make it last.

CONCLUSION

You've worked hard to create a space that truly reflects your needs, values, and vision. The organized, clutter-free environment you've crafted adds an aesthetic touch. It also sets the foundation for a life of ease, productivity, and calm. It's the result of intentional effort, careful planning, and consistent habits. But remember, this isn't the end; it's just the beginning. Living in harmony with your space is a continuous process, one that evolves as you do.

Embracing the ongoing process of decluttering is key to maintaining the balance you've achieved. Decluttering is about making mindful decisions and staying connected to what truly adds value to your life. Over time, you'll find that letting go of excess stuff becomes easier and that staying organized feels more natural. Each time you make space for what matters most, you're reinforcing your commitment to living a life of purpose and clarity. Don't be hard on yourself if things get messy again; life happens, and it's a part of the process. The important thing is that you've developed the skills and mindset to reset and continue on your journey.

As you move forward, remind yourself that resources are available to guide you in your ongoing journey of organization and well-being. If you're ever feeling stuck, or if you just need inspiration to keep going, turn to *Declutter Your Home* for fresh perspectives and new strategies. They can offer the advice or motivation needed to get you back on track when life gets busy.

Lastly, know that you are in control. You've created a space that supports your goals and reflects your journey. Now, it's up to you to maintain it, knowing that every effort, no matter how small, counts. Celebrate your successes, big and small, and allow yourself to enjoy the peace and clarity that come with living in harmony with your surroundings.

If you've enjoyed the journey to a clutter-free home and found the tips and strategies in this book helpful, I would love to hear from you! Your feedback means the world and helps me continue to create content that supports and empowers others. Please take a moment to leave a review and share how this book has made a difference in your life. Your thoughts and experiences can inspire others to take the first step toward an organized and stress-free home. Thank you for being part of this journey!

Keep moving forward with confidence. The progress you've made is a testament to your dedication, and the ongoing process of living in an organized, decluttered space will only continue to serve you as you grow and evolve. You're not just transforming your home—you're transforming your life. Embrace it fully, and let each day bring new opportunities for improvement, joy, and peace. You've got this.

THE ULTIMATE HOME DECLUTTERING CHECKLIST

EMOTIONAL ATTACHMENTS TO POSSESSIONS

☐ Reflect on why certain items are hard to let go of (sentimental value, guilt, etc.).

☐ Practice gratitude for the memories attached to items without needing to hold onto them.

☐ Challenge thoughts of "I might need it someday" and remind yourself that you are creating space for what truly matters.

PERSONALIZED DECLUTTERING PLAN

☐ Walk through each room in your home and assess which areas need the most attention.

☐ Take photos of each space to track your progress visually.

☐ Prioritize spaces based on frequency of use and impact on your productivity and mood.

☐ Break your decluttering plan into manageable tasks and set realistic timelines for each.

LIVING ROOM ORGANIZATION

☐ Remove unnecessary items such as outdated décor, magazines, and unused electronics.

☐ Group similar items together (e.g., books, remote controls, DVDs).

☐ Choose décor that brings joy and serves a purpose, opting for multi-functional furniture.

☐ Keep surfaces clean and uncluttered to promote a calming atmosphere.

☐ Experiment with furniture placement to enhance the space's flow, encouraging relaxation and connection.

KITCHEN STREAMLINING

☐ Declutter kitchen drawers and cabinets by removing duplicate or seldom-used items.

☐ Keep only essential kitchen tools easily accessible.

☐ Organize the pantry by grouping similar items together (e.g., spices, canned goods).

☐ Label containers and shelves to ensure everything has its place.

☐ Set up a meal prep-friendly kitchen with designated areas for planning and prepping meals.

BEDROOM SIMPLIFICATION

☐ Simplify your wardrobe by keeping only clothing that fits, is in good condition, and is worn regularly.

☐ Donate or discard clothing items that no longer serve a purpose.

☐ Create a restful bedroom environment by incorporating soothing colors and minimal décor.

☐ Implement a calming nighttime routine to promote better rest and relaxation.

☐ Organize your closet with a capsule wardrobe to simplify clothing choices.

Home Office Organization

☐ Declutter your workspace by removing non-essential items from your desk.

☐ Set up designated spaces for office supplies, files, and electronics to improve productivity.

☐ Clean up your computer files by organizing or deleting outdated documents.

☐ Unsubscribe from unnecessary emails and delete unused apps to reduce digital clutter.

☐ Set up an ergonomic and inspiring workspace to encourage comfort and creativity.

BATHROOM SIMPLIFICATION

☐ Declutter personal care items by removing expired products and consolidating duplicates.

☐ Keep only essentials visible, storing extras out of sight to reduce visual clutter.

☐ Maintain a clean and inviting bathroom by wiping down surfaces regularly.

☐ Organize toiletries in baskets, bins, or cabinets for easy access.

☐ Develop a minimalist bathroom routine by choosing quality personal care products and creating a cleaning schedule.

PAPER CLUTTER MANAGEMENT

☐ Implement an effective filing system by sorting documents into categories (e.g., bills, receipts, warranties).

☐ Create a filing system that is easy to maintain and stay consistent with.

☐ Reduce paper clutter by scanning important documents and storing them digitally on a cloud-based system.

☐ Opt for paperless billing and subscription services to minimize physical mail.

☐ Set up a paper management system with designated areas for sorting and filing documents on a daily or weekly basis.

MAINTAINING YOUR ORGANIZED HOME

☐ Establish daily and weekly routines for light tidying up to keep your space clutter-free.

☐ Create a weekly cleaning and decluttering schedule to stay on top of maintenance tasks.

☐ Involve family members by assigning age-appropriate tasks for everyone to help maintain the home.

☐ Encourage each person to keep their personal space organized and contribute to maintaining shared spaces.

☐ Create a personalized checklist of daily, weekly, and monthly tasks to stay on track.

CELEBRATING YOUR SUCCESS

☐ Reflect on your journey of transformation and recognize the hard work you've put in.

☐ Celebrate your progress, no matter how small, and take time to appreciate your organized space.

☐ Revisit your home organization goals periodically and adjust them based on changing needs and circumstances.

☐ Design a gratitude ritual to honor the peaceful, clutter-free environment you've created, perhaps with a small weekly cleaning or organizing habit.

☐ Create a ritual to celebrate your new lifestyle, whether it's a simple acknowledgment of your achievements or a more formal end-of-week routine.

REFERENCES

Burkeman, O. (2017, May 5). *Will you regret later what you're doing now? Don't even think about it*. The Guardian. https://www.theguardian.com/lifeandstyle/2017/may/05/stop-worrying-about-future-regrets-change-your-life-oliver-burkeman

Coren, M. J. (2023, September 27). *How to keep junk snail mail out of your mailbox forever*. The Washington Post. https://www.washingtonpost.com/climate-environment/2023/09/26/how-to-stop-junk-mail/

How to stay active at home & improve your mental health during crisis. (2022, April 16). *Long Island Health Collaborative*. https://www.lihealthcollab.org/news-and-blog/your-at-home-wellness-plan-how-to-stay-active--mentally-fit

Sander, L. (2019, January 25). *What does clutter do to your brain and body?* NewsGP. https://www1.racgp.org.au/newsgp/clinical/what-does-clutter-do-to-your-brain-and-body

Sethi, C. (2024, October 18). *Capsule wardrobes for streamlined decision-making*. LinkedIn. https://www.linkedin.com/pulse/capsule-wardrobes-streamlined-decision-making-cassandra-sethi-wtf2c

Song, I., Baek, K., Kim, C., & Song, C. (2023). Effects of nature sounds on the attention and physiological and psychological relaxation. *Urban Forestry & Urban Greening, 86*, 127987–127987. https://doi.org/10.1016/j.ufug.2023.127987

Space Refinery. (2024, April 30). *Colors psychology: How to choose the right colors for your workspace*. Space Refinery. https://www.spacerefinery.com/blog/colors-psychology-guide

Yetman, D. (2024, October 22). *Best color of light for sleep: What works for adults and kids*. Healthline. https://www.healthline.com/health/best-color-light-for-sleep

IMAGE REFERENCES

Alanajordan. (2024). *Bedroom cozy vintage books bed* [Image]. Pixabay. https://pixabay.com/illustrations/bedroom-cozy-vintage-books-bed-8902277/

Alperomeresin. (2023). *Messy mess stress depressive* [Image]. Pixabay. https://pixabay.com/illustrations/messy-mess-stress-depressive-8131397/

Andersen, A. (2019). *White ipad* [Image]. Pexels. https://www.pexels.com/photo/white-ipad-2351844/

Banks, C. (2024). *A bedroom with a bed dresser and a window* [Image]. Unsplash. https://unsplash.com/photos/a-bedroom-with-a-bed-dresser-and-a-window-r8i3RwrVcRk

Congerdesign. (2024). *Clean rag cleaning rags household* [Image]. Pixabay. https://pixabay.com/photos/clean-rag-cleaning-rags-household-571679/

Fill. (2016). *Paper shredder flakes recycling* [Image]. Pixabay. https://pixabay.com/photos/paper-shredder-flakes-recycling-1392749/

Flowerfield. (2022). *Computer os folder design desktop* [Image]. Pixabay. https://pixabay.com/vectors/computer-os-folder-design-desktop-7400014/

Hassan, M. (2022a). *Checklist to do list business form* [Image]. Pixabay. https://pixabay.com/illustrations/checklist-to-do-list-business-form-7325314/

Hassan, M. (2022b). *Mind clean brain psychology* [Image]. Pixabay. https://pixabay.com/vectors/mind-clean-brain-psychology-7670201/

Henderson, G. (2018). *Today I am grateful book* [Image]. Unsplash. https://unsplash.com/photos/today-i-am-grateful-book-M4lve6jR26E

Hoekstra, R. (2020). *Computer desk desk office marketing* [Image]. Pixabay. https://pixabay.com/vectors/computer-desk-desk-office-marketing-7339325/

Jessica Lewis the paintedsquare (2023). *Baskets with laundry standing on the floor by the bed..* [Image]. Pexels. https://www.pexels.com/photo/baskets-with-laundry-standing-on-the-floor-by-the-bed-18063446/

Muradi. (2020). *Brown wooden shelf with assorted spices* [Image]. Unsplash. https://unsplash.com/photos/brown-wooden-shelf-with-assorted-spices-0b8NaL2CMaQ

Piacquadio, A. (2020). *Daily chores of a mother* [Image]. Pexels. https://www.pexels.com/photo/daily-chores-of-a-mother-3768910/

Pixabay. (2016). *Gray wooden sideboard* [Image]. Pexels. https://www.pexels.com/photo/gray-wooden-sideboard-271816/

Production, M. (2021). *White ceramic vase on the tray* [Image]. Pexels. https://www.pexels.com/photo/white-ceramic-vase-on-the-tray-8217302/

Tookapic. (2015). *Office work desk computer* [Image]. Pixabay. https://pixabay.com/photos/office-work-desk-computer-932926/

Vakhtbovycn, M. (2021). *Room with mirrors and chandeliers* [Image]. Pexels. https://www.pexels.com/photo/room-with-mirrors-and-chandeliers-8092190/

Winkler, M. (2020). *Green typewriter on brown wooden table* [Image]. Pexels. https://www.pexels.com/photo/green-typewriter-on-brown-wooden-table-4052198/

Zvolskiy, D. (2019). *Chopping boards near oven under hood* [Image]. Pexels. https://www.pexels.com/photo/chopping-boards-near-oven-under-hood-2062426/

www.ingramcontent.com/pod-product-compliance
Lightning Source LLC
Chambersburg PA
CBHW071225090426
42736CB00014B/2979

9 798897 540013